ENGLAND RUGBY

Also by Barry Bowker:

North Midlands Rugby
Sixty Years of Old Boys Rugger

England Rugby

A History of the National Side, 1871–1978

Barry Bowker

Revised Edition

With a foreword by
M. R. Steele-Bodger

CASSELL
London

CASSELL LTD.
35 Red Lion Square, London WC1R 4SG
and at Sydney, Auckland, Toronto, Johannesburg,
an affiliate of
Macmillan Publishing Co., Inc.,
New York

First edition 1976
Second edition 1978

ISBN 0 304 30214 7

Printed and bound in Great Britain at
The Camelot Press Ltd, Southampton

778

Dedicated to England's Rugby Footballers

Fourteen Triple Crowns
Seven Grand Slams
The only home country to beat both New Zealand and South Africa
The only home country to beat South Africa home and away
The only home country to beat New Zealand home and away
Winners of the only World 'Sevens'

Contents

Illustrations

Between pp. 66 and 67

Between pp. 130 and 131

Foreword to the First Edition

By M. R. Steele-Bodger
(England Representative on the International Rugby Football Board and past President of the Rugby Football Union)

I was not really surprised when Barry Bowker told me that he was writing a history of England International Rugby which would cover the whole period of its development from the earliest organized beginnings as a national side right up to the present day. I was not surprised because the author is almost what might be called a 'natural' for such an undertaking. Firstly, he is a graduate historian with that love of researching and attention to detail so often associated with such a qualification. Secondly, although interested in all sport, he is an ardent devotee of rugby football who has over many years been an enthusiastic and hardworking administrator for the game in the Midlands area. Thirdly, he is an Englishman and unashamedly proud of his heritage and of the sporting achievements of his fellow countrymen, one of whom at Rugby School created the game while others by their deeds and ability on the playing field have made England's record in international rugby football the outstanding one that it is.

The various chapters in the book cover in chronological stages all England's international matches from 1871 to 1976. As one would have expected over such a long span of time there have been periods when England teams swept all before them and other times that could be described, at best, as lean periods. With the present national side having had a poor season, it is comforting to recall that only recently have England achieved the supreme success of defeating the three major rugby-playing countries of the Southern Hemisphere and all within the space of eighteen months. Victories over South Africa and New Zealand on their own grounds and over Australia at Twickenham constitute, within that time limit, a record that will probably never be equalled and would on its own be a fit subject for a book.

This book is so full of facts that it might have read like a catalogue. Mr Bowker, however, has avoided this trap by introducing little known but interesting stories about the great players and important incidents that he is describing. In this way interest is maintained and the gradual evolution of the present game is revealed as having occurred in a progressive pattern. Those who currently disagree with one or other of the existing laws will be able to trace back to the time when a particular facet of play necessitated the introduction of that law in order that the game as a whole could preserve a balance between three-quarter and forward play.

It is intriguing to discover that England were deprived of yet another record by the decision of the referee in 1881 when he ruled that a pass thrown half the width of the field was not football and in some manner ungentlemanly. As a result England were limited to thirteen tries in that match—their first against Wales—a record which they have to share with South Africa, who dealt equally harshly with France in 1907.

During the hundred years and more that international rugby has been played there have almost inevitably been times when umbrage was taken and sometimes this led to the cancellation of fixtures. The first such occasion was in 1884, and if only the modern advantage law had been in operation then there would have been no dispute and England would not have been ostracized later from international competition for two years.

A whole chapter is devoted to the golden era of the early 1920s, and quite rightly so. The names of that time are legendary. W. J. A. Davies, whose international record of only one defeat in 22 appearances is unchallenged, and his scrum half partner, C. A. Kershaw, were surely the most successful pair of halves any country ever had. C. N. Lowe, that great wing, scored eighteen tries in twenty-five appearances, which compares more than favourably with D. J. Duckham's modern-day tally of ten tries in thirty-six games.

I enjoyed the thought of Tucker, way back in 1930, being summoned by the selectors to charter a plane so as to get to

Cardiff in time. And who was the full-back from Gloucester brought into the national side after six years without playing in a trial who kicked the match-winning goals and proved himself to be an inspired selection? Who was the last player to be capped for England directly from an Old Boys Club? The book brings many such facts to light and such is Mr Bowker's reputation for accuracy that I have no hesitation in believing him. That applies even when he states that Travers played as an emergency full-back for only the last ten minutes of the match against Wales in 1948. I played in that match and, no doubt due to the pressure we were under, remember it as being at least twice as long!

I am sure that this book has a place in the library of any rugby player and Barry Bowker is to be congratulated and thanked for the hours of research that have made it possible. In the course of this research many errors in previous records have been corrected and from a rugby historian's point of view that alone is worth while. Apart from that it will be a help in settling more speedily and amicably than is usual those inevitable club house disagreements over facts and figures.

March 1976 M. R. STEELE-BODGER

Author's Note

The idea of this book was born in conversations I had with the late Commander W. J. A. Davies, England's greatest player.

My thanks are due to Mr M. R. Steele-Bodger, England representative on the International Rugby Football Board, for writing the Foreword; to the many internationals who have answered my queries; to Mr Geoff Adams, Chief Librarian of the *Birmingham Post and Mail*, for permission to research in their archives; to my colleague Mrs Marion Davis for expert secretarial assistance; and to my friend Keith Hatter for his patience and advice at all stages.

Especial help with photographs has been given by Mrs Peggy Davies, widow of W. J. A., and by Mr Alfred Wright, keeper of the Rugby Football Union records at Twickenham.

The information in this book is complete up to March 1978.

Chapter One

The Shoving Age 1871–6

The first Rugby football international was Scotland versus England at Raeburn Place, Edinburgh, on 27 March 1871.

It took place because the Football Association had arranged an 'international' between England and 'Scotland' in 1870 and had picked both sides themselves. The 'Scottish' side was confined to men living in England, and it was claimed that the only qualification some of them had to play for Scotland was a liking for Scotch whisky.

Many of the leading Scottish clubs played Rugby and they were so incensed that a football international should be soccer, and not the game they played, that they issued a challenge for a twenty-a-side match between England and Scotland under Rugby School laws.

The Football Association had been founded in 1863, but it had been rather a matter of pride amongst the Rugby-playing fraternity that, thanks to their strict off-side laws and their complete ban on passing forward, their game had been comparatively free of the disputes that necessitate a governing body.

The Rugby Football Union was not founded until 26 January 1871, and it was Blackheath, as the oldest open club in London (founded 1858), who accepted the Scottish challenge. A committee was formed to select the players and decide on the colours—a white jersey with a large red rose on the left breast.

No Woolwich Academy players and only one from Richmond (founded 1861) could make the journey, but Manchester (founded 1860) and Liverpool (1857) supplied four and three men respectively to give the impression that a truly national side was being fielded. There is little doubt that the northerners were recommended by A. Lyon and J. H. Clayton, who were among the ten men in this first England team who had been to Rugby School and may be presumed to have learnt the game properly:

A. G. Guillemard (West Kent), A. Lyon (Liverpool), R. R. Osborne (Manchester) *backs*; W. MacLaren (Manchester) *three-quarter*; J. E. Bentley (Gipsies), F. Tobin (Liverpool), J. F. Green (West Kent) *half-backs*; F. Stokes, B. H. Burns, C. A. Crompton, C. W. Sherrard (all Blackheath), R. H. Birkett (Clapham Rovers), A. Davenport, J. M. Dugdale (both Ravenscourt Park), A. S. Gibson, H. J. C. Turner (both Manchester), A. St. G. Hamersley (Marlborough Nomads), J. H. Luscombe (Gipsies), J. H. Clayton (Liverpool), D. P. Turner (Richmond) *forwards*.

England's captain in this and the next two seasons was Frederick Stokes, an Old Rugbeian and the Blackheath skipper. He was regarded as one of the best examples of a heavy forward, always on the ball and first rate in the thick of the scrummage.

For this was the shoving age of Rugby football. The ideal scrum was when the thirteen-man pack was compact, with every man pressing firmly on the man in front of him, bodies and legs close together, so as to form a firmly packed mass to resist the weight of a like mass of opponents. The scrum was defined as taking place when 'all who have closed round on their respective sides endeavour to push their opponents back and by kicking the ball to drive it in the direction of the opposite goal-line'. The twenty-six heavyweights would lean up against each other for periods of up to five minutes encouraged by remarks from the three half-backs such as 'Steady with it', 'Not too fast' and 'Keep it together'.

Scrummaging at this time meant carrying the pack by superior weight; a scrum was a prolonged trial of strength cheered by spectators as though they were watching a tug of war. Heeling out was considered to be bad form, because the forwards in front of the ball were technically offside and obstructing the play.

The halves stood five or six yards from the scrum, as, if they were too near, they had less time to pick up the ball when it had been kicked through the scrum by their opponents. They then had to gather before the opposing forwards, who had driven through, could take it on and were expected to be expert 'dodgers' and strong runners. They played for themselves and ran with the ball under one arm ready to hand off. Passing was regarded as funking. The laws of the time recommended no dimensions for the field of play, and the Englishmen were aghast to find the Raeburn Place pitch in 1871 only fifty-five yards wide. This meant that their halves kept on 'dodging' their way into touch, whence the ball was returned into play by a player (a) bounding it out and then running with it or kicking it or throwing it back to his own side, (b) throwing it at right angles to the forwards bunched on the touch-line, or (c) walking out with it any distance not less than five or more than fifteen yards and putting it down (for a scrum), first declaring how far he intended to walk out.

The sole three-quarter had to cover the entire field between the three halves and the three full-backs. He was seldom troubled by forwards and rarely had to drop on. He had to be a good tackler, as he was the first line of defence against halves who had broken through. Sometimes a wild kick through would give him the chance to drop for goal. He was not expected to run with the ball, and of the ten tries scored by England in twenty-a-side internationals, six were obtained by forwards and four by halves. The full-backs guarded the goal line. Their duties were purely defensive and the best exponents had to be good at tackling and dropping for touch—punting was frowned on and reckoned to be the inferior method of gaining ground.

Proof of the popularity of the game in Scotland was that 4,000 spectators attended the first international, though rugby must have been a very dull game to watch.

This first international was fifty minutes each way and the first half was evenly contested. The Scots then drove the ball over the line from a five-yard scrum and touched down. At this time umpires only acted if there was an appeal. The English claimed that the ball had never been in the scrum properly, but the umpire allowed the try at goal as so many Englishmen were appealing instead of just the captain as was usual! Up to 1875 matches were decided by a majority of goals only and F. Cross (Merchistonians) landed the all-important conversion.

England replied with its first-ever try, by R. H. Birkett—in the corner and too far out for Stokes to convert.

R. H. Birkett had a remarkable sporting history. He played

rugby for England as both a forward and a three-quarter; he played twice in the same England team as his brother and had a son who captained England. R. H. Birkett played for Clapham Rovers, who had the distinction of being a dual soccer and rugger club, and, as a goal-keeper, he won a soccer cap for England *v.* Scotland in 1879 and an F.A. Cup Winner's medal in 1880.

Cross scored Scotland's second try after an unintentional knock-on by one of his own side (quite legal). He failed with the conversion, so Scotland won by one goal and one try to one try or, as some papers of the time put it, by one goal to nil.

The Rugby Football Union had been founded too late to organize the first international, although of course it has been responsible for all subsequent England teams.

The first Scottish match under its auspices was in 1872 at Kennington Oval where a pitch 120 yards by 70 had been marked out. The Oval was indeed the English sporting Mecca at this time. England played both rugger and soccer internationals there, and in 1880 it was the venue of the first home cricket Test.

The England XX contained only six of the previous side—Stokes, Guillemard, Bentley, Sherrard, Hamersley and D. P. Turner. It is significant that there were no men from Manchester or Liverpool; northern clubs had decided to remain aloof from the new Union. In fact the 1872 England side was chosen only from clubs affiliated to the R.F.U. This meant that Oxford and Cambridge men, though the first Varsity match was played that spring, had to be nominated by their vacation clubs. Thus W. O. Moberley, the Oxford captain, and F. W. Isherwood, their best forward, appeared under the banner of Ravenscourt Park, a club to which most metroplitan Old Rugbeians belonged. Alumni of another good rugger school, Tonbridge, were to be found with the Gipsies, who supplied J. E. Bentley, a strong, fast half, J. A. Body, a pocket Hercules of a forward, and F. Luscombe, who had convinced Stokes the previous year that it was his duty as captain of the senior club to accept the Scottish challenge. The first of the genuine Old Boys clubs, however, was Marlborough Nomads (founded 1868); they had F. W. Mills at back, H. Freeman at three-quarter and F. I. Currey and A. St. G. Hamersley in the pack. At half was P. Wilkinson from

Harlequins (founded 1866) but listed as 'Law Club' because the 'Quins were little known. Guy's Hospital, founded 1843 and the oldest Rugby club in the world, supplied W. W. Pinching, a forward, to England's first international side to play at home.

England won by two goals (one dropped) and two tries to one dropped goal. The first try was scored by Hamersley after a short 'maul in goal'. Only those players who were touching the ball with their hands when it crossed the goal-line might continue in the maul in goal, and when a player had once released his hold of the ball after it was inside the goal-line he might not again join in the maul. If he attempted to do so he might be dragged out by the opposite side! This law persisted until 1892, and there was one famous occasion when two men (cheered on by their fellow players and the spectators) had a maul in goal which lasted five minutes. Isherwood converted Hamersley's try to record England's first goal. The second half was notable for England's first dropped goal—by Freeman, performing one of the functions expected of a top-class three-quarter, and for the first try by a back, S. H. Finney, from the Engineering College at Coopers Hill, running in. Coopers Hill were one of the strongest teams in England and Finney was the crack half-back of the era, being especially good at rushing through a crowd of opponents when close to goal. It was written of him that towards the end of a hard match he generally wore the appearance of having been engaged in a prize fight, but the more wounds he received the better he seemed to play.

The 1873 match on the West of Scotland ground at Partick was a goalless draw but is memorable for two off-the-field incidents. Before the match, the England captain ordered his team to have leather bars fixed to the soles of their boots because the pitch was so slippery. When the canny Scottish cobbler had finished, two of the English backs were each minus a boot and one of them had to play in a dress boot. After the match, the Englishmen so enjoyed themselves—and who was to stop them? (travelling expenses were not paid until 1880 and hotel expenses later still)—that in the early hours an English forward was found driving one of Her Majesty's mail carts in the middle of Glasgow. He very nearly found that 'run in' did not mean the same to a constable as to a Rugby umpire!

By 1873 some northern clubs had joined the R.F.U., and in 1874 the first trial between the North and the South was played at Rugby. Though the South scored three tries to the North's one, the game was a draw as only goals counted. Manchester and Liverpool, who ran the Lancashire county team between them (Lancashire had first played Yorkshire in 1870, before England first played Scotland), contributed four of England's 1874 XX. One was Liverpool's E. Kewley, who was to gain seven caps and become the first from a northern club to skipper England, and another was Manchester's Roger Walker, also a forward, who played five times for England. The 1874 international was notable for a last-minute dropped goal by Freeman which beat Scotland's only score—a try.

Ireland was admitted to international status in 1875 and came to the Oval. It transpired that there were two rival Unions who each sent ten men and it is not surprising that England won comfortably by two goals (one dropped) and one try to nil. The Hospitals Cup was inaugurated in 1875: and for England this year Guy's (the first winners) provided A. W. Pearson, a steady back and good place kick, and St George's (the first runners-up) W. E. Collins, a plucky half.

The Irish match also saw the first international appearance of a man from a Yorkshire club—W. H. Hutchinson, the Hull and county captain, a fine strapping forward known as 'the Baron'.

For the Scottish fixture it was back to Raeburn Place. This time the pitch was eighty-five yards wide, so narrowness could not be offered as the reason for the 0–0 draw. It is recorded that the dropping of both sides was brilliant and that on half a dozen occasions a foot the other way would have caused the downfall of one goal or the other. With dropping such an integral part of the old game and practised so much, one is left to wonder why England had only three successful drops for goal in its first eight years. This match marked the last appearance of Richmond's D. P. Turner, a desperately hard-working forward always keen and untiring and 'as regardless of danger as an Irishman'; he was the only man to have played in all England's first six internationals.

F. Luscombe, too, brought his total of caps to six in 1875–6 when he was honoured with England's captaincy and both Scotland and Ireland were defeated in a single season for the first time. Another stalwart forward in his last season was the giant J. A. Bush of Clifton, which, founded in 1872, was then regarded as the strongest club in the South outside London. Bush played for England five times; he missed the 1873–4 season because he was keeping wicket for W. G. Grace's team in Australia.

Ireland were beaten by a goal and a try to nil in Dublin, and Scotland were defeated by the same score at the Oval. The goal against Scotland really heralded a new era. W. C. Hutchinson (Coopers Hill) passed his opposing half-backs by sheer pace and had run 100 yards before, being an unselfish player, he transferred to F. H. Lee (Oxford University), a forward who believed in the new 'following-up'. Lee ran in behind the posts and L. Stokes (Blackheath), to become known as the most scientific player of his age, converted the try to register the first of his many goals for England in his second international.

Chapter Two

The Loose Game 1877–82

It was 1892 before a Law stated that 'The game should be played by fifteen players on each side', and as late as 1882 an English trial match—Oxford and Cambridge combined *v.* London—was sixteen a side, mainly, it must be admitted, because each university wanted equal representation. However, in 1875 Oxford *v.* Cambridge was reduced from twenty to fifteen a side, and Scotland proposed fifteen a side for internationals.

The Rugby Football Union demurred for a year but on 5 February 1877 England fielded its first international XV—against Ireland at The Oval. The team was:

L. Birkett (Clapham Rovers), L. Stokes (Blackheath) *backs*; R. H. Birkett (Clapham Rovers), A. N. Hornby (Preston Grasshoppers) *three-quarters*; W. C. Hutchinson, P. L. Price (both Coopers Hill) *halves*; E. Kewley (Liverpool, capt.), F. R. Adams (Richmond), R. H. Fowler (Leeds), G. Harrison (Hull), W. H. Hunt (Preston Grasshoppers), F. H. Lee (Oxford University), M. W. Marshall (Blackheath), C. J. C. Touzell (Cambridge University), E. B. Turner (St George's Hospital) *forwards*.

Instead of thirteen or fourteen forwards on each side there were now only nine or ten. The forwards were no longer handicapped by superfluous numbers and began to take a part in open play. The old standing up and blind shoving often did more harm than good, as forwards had no idea where the ball was, so they started to scrum with their heads down and control the destination of the ball. The object of possession became not to keep the ball tight but to wheel the scrum and have a combined foot-rush downfield. This loose game was encouraged by a change of law in 1878 by which a player had to put the ball down immediately he was held, and requirements for top-class forwards henceforth included close dribbling, fast following-up and short passing to the open side.

Some of the forwards like Blackheath's M. W. Marshall, one of three Old Wellingtonians who captained England in the 1870s (Hon. H. A. Lawrence and F. R. Adams, both Richmond, were the others) and the England record-holder with ten caps when he retired in 1878, shone at both the shoving and loose games, but there was now a place in the pack for small, thick-set forwards who owed no reputation to their weight. As early as 1878 two Blackheath men, G. W. Burton and A. J. Budd, were described as 'playing on the verge of the scrum' (the original wing forwards!) and Blackheath were one of the clubs who claimed to have invented the fast forward game. They certainly perfected it and in 1879–80 had an unbeaten season (P. 16, W. 14, D. 2). Their captain from 1876 to 1881, a period when they lost only six matches, was Lennard Stokes, the best three-quarter of his day. As Montague Shearman wrote: 'There have been more brilliant runners and safer tacklers, but probably no better drop-kick and none with more judgement and knowledge of the game. His command over the ball in drop-kicking was marvellous and his drops at goal and long drops into touch were masterpieces. One great element in his success was the careful eye he kept on his halves and backs to ensure a safe defence of the field.'

For the advent of the loose forwards had brought changes in back play. The halves were no longer the glory boys who could abscond with the ball while the forwards shoved each other. The best halves now were defensive, able to whip up the ball in the face of the forward rushes and able to tackle the biggest forward who had the ball in his hand. England had replaced one of the three full-backs with a second three-quarter because the goal-line was too far back for three to hold as a last line of defence, and the three-quarters now became the men who ran in the spectacular tries.

In fact the 1877 Irish match saw England's first try by a three-quarter—A. N. Hornby. Hornby had been to Harrow School, had not taken up the Rugby game until relatively late in life and was thirty when he won his first cap. He and three brothers Hunt all played for England from the Preston

Grasshoppers club, which had been founded in 1869, but later they all found their way into the Manchester club. Hornby was even better known as a cricketer, and in 1882 became the first man to captain England concurrently at both cricket and rugby. England beat Ireland by two goals and a try to nil in 1877 but lost to Scotland by a dropped goal to nil.

The Scottish match of 1878 was a scoreless draw, it being recorded that 'Adams made a good run-in for England, but it was given up as the Scots were at a disadvantage owing to a misconception of one of the laws'. A notable debut was that of E. Temple Gurdon (Richmond) who went on to establish the then English record of sixteen caps by the time he last played in 1886. Gurdon's speciality was 'working' the ball with his feet and keeping it when the scrum gave or twisted. Often a scrum would scatter past him, and when it had gone by there was Gurdon speeding away from them with the ball still in front of him. A similar type of forward was G. Thomson, who helped Halifax beat York in the first Yorkshire Cup Final in 1878. G. F. Vernon (Blackheath), another 1878 debutant, was clever at getting the ball when it was thrown out of touch—one of the first line-out experts, though his aim would be to drop the ball and try to dribble through. That he was a good ball player can be imagined from the fact that he later played Test cricket for England.

The next week Ireland were beaten in Dublin by two goals and a try to nil, one of England's tries being scored by W. J. Penny (King's College), the first try from full-back in international rugger.

The 1879 game with Scotland was the first for the Calcutta Cup, presented by the Calcutta (India) Club on its dissolution 'as an International Challenge Cup to be played for annually by England and Scotland'. G. W. Burton, already known as 'very fast in the open and a great scorer', ran in and Stokes converted. Scotland replied with a dropped goal—enough to draw the match, for although since 1875 matches had been decided by tries, it was only if no goals were scored or the goals were equal, and at this time a dropped goal was as good as a goal from try, or from a mark (penalty goals could not be kicked in international matches until 1892). Stokes had two conversions and a drop in the 'three goals' win over Ireland.

The 1880 season saw England win both its internationals for the first time since the change from XXs to XVs. The new captain was L. Stokes, but the R.F.U. had a job to field a representative side in Ireland and only six men played in both matches. Ireland scored its first try against England but after the interval England ran in twice and Stokes converted one.

The Scottish match was played at Manchester on account of poor attendances at the Oval. Before the interval, half-back H. H. Taylor (St George's Hospital) justified his reputation for spotting a gap with two short but brilliant 'runs-in'. After half time Scotland scored a converted try, but England added tries by T. Fry (Queen's House), E. T. Gurdon and Burton, two converted by Stokes.

Fry was the sole full-back, and from this time England had one full-back only, there being ten forwards. 'Queen's House' was the club of Rowland Hill, one of the stalwarts of the R.F.U. in whose memory gates were erected and an England–Wales *v.* Scotland–Ireland match was staged at Twickenham in 1929. Hill had been born at Queen's House, the royal palace in Greenwich, and 'Queen's House' was one of several London clubs which had turned out internationals but were dissolved in the 1880s. Most of them fielded one team only and played on commons: as their founder members retired and as it became necessary for clubs to find private grounds, they were wound up.

The year 1881 started with victory by two goals and two tries to nil over Ireland at Manchester, H. H. Taylor, then listed as Blackheath, becoming the first man to score three tries in a match for England and W. R. Richardson (Manchester Grammar School) the first schoolboy to play for England.

Taylor's record lasted only a fortnight because G. W. Burton notched four against Wales. England consented to play Wales 'to set a good example to the other nationalities'. The venue was Mr Richardson's field, Blackheath's ground between their leaving the Heath in 1877 and settling at Rectory Field in 1883. England won by seven goals, one dropped goal, six tries to nil (69–0 translated into modern scoring values). The thirteen tries were scored by Burton (four), H. Vassall (three), A. J. Budd, C. W. L. Fernandes, H. C. Rowley, H. H. Taylor, R. Hunt, and H. T. Twynam (one each). Stokes converted six and Hunt converted one and dropped a goal. There would have been fourteen tries, but when Stokes threw the ball half-way across the ground to Hunt, who ran in easily, the ball was ordered back by the umpires: such a long pass was not football! If this fourteenth 'try' had been allowed, England alone would hold the record for most tries in an international. As it is, they share the distinction with South Africa, who scored thirteen against France in 1907.

The Scottish match at Raeburn Place was memorable because England arrived with fourteen men only, Taylor having missed the night mail. F. T. Wright, a Manchester lad studying in Edinburgh, was enlisted to play half-back with H. Campbell Rowley (Manchester), who had played in the pack against Ireland and Wales. However, Rowley played the game of his life, drawing attention from the weaker side, closely marking A. R. Don Wauchope (one of Scotland's greatest halves) and scoring England's try. Stokes, in his twelfth and last international, dropped a goal which travelled '80 yards from kick to pitch', but Scotland drew level by means of an unconverted try and a converted one.

After the 1881 débâcle Wales were given matches against North of England and Midland Counties in 1882, when England failed to win an international for the first time since 1873. Charles Gurdon (Richmond), brother of Temple and larger—at thirteen and a half stone he was, by the standards of the day, massive—was captain in Dublin where each side scored two tries. At Manchester Scotland won by two tries to nil and thus became the first side in the England–Scotland series to win away from home. This was the first international to have a neutral referee as well as umpires.

England's poor form this season was attributed to their want of condition and lack of combination. Fortunately one of their forwards, H. ('Jumbo') Vassall, was captain of Oxford University in 1881 and 1882 and was developing revolutionary ideas based on training and teamwork.

Chapter Three

The First Triple Crowns 1883–7

England started the season 1882–3 with victory by two goals and four tries to nil over Wales at Swansea. The winning team was:

A. S. Taylor (Blackheath); W. N. Bolton (R.M.C. Sandhurst), A. M. Evanson, G. C. Wade; A. Rotherham (all Oxford University), J. H. Payne (Broughton); E. T. Gurdon (Richmond, capt.), H. Vassall, W. M. Tatham, C. S. Wooldridge, R. S. Kindersley (all Oxford University), H. G. Fuller (Cambridge University), R. S. F. Henderson, G. Standing (both Blackheath), G. T. Thomson (Halifax).

Wade scored three tries, Thomson, Henderson and Bolton one each, Evanson converting two.

For the Irish match at Manchester H. T. Twynam (Richmond) substituted for Rotherham at half, and B. B. Middleton (Birkenhead Park), R. M. Pattisson (Cambridge University) and E. G. Moore (Oxford University) came into the pack. Tatham, Wade, Bolton and Twynam scored tries, one converted by Evanson. Ireland replied with a try.

For the Scottish game at Raeburn Place, H. B. Tristram (Oxford University) replaced the injured Taylor, setting a new standard of full-back play, and C. Gurdon (Richmond) was recalled for what was still the big match of the season—and was to remain so for many years. C. Reid, the 'champion forward' of Scotland in the process of earning his twenty caps, obtained a try for his country, but Rotherham and Bolton both scored for England.

England had won in Scotland for the first time. For the first time a home country had beaten all the other three in the same season and England could thus claim to be the first winners of the 'Triple Crown'—though such a term was not heard of yet. England's victory was hailed as a triumph for scientific combination over determined forward play.

This England team had a distinctive style—the Oxford passing inaugurated by Harry Vassall—and before long passing was all the fashion. An observer in 1887 wrote, 'If one comes on to a field before play has commenced, the men waiting for the game are not taking drop-kick practice, or dribbling the ball, as was their wont before the rage for passing came in, but are now seen playing at catch-ball and slinging the ball from hand to hand, not high in the air, but about the level of the hands from the ground.'

By 1881 it had become tacitly accepted that heeling from the scrum was legal. Vassall encouraged this tactic and made his halves, who played right and left, pass to a three-quarter by sweeping the ball off the ground into the hands of the destined recipient in one movement.

In Alan Rotherham he had the player to put his theories into practice. Rotherham had been to Uppingham, which played its own brand of football, yet within two years of leaving school he was a key man in the England XV, passing before he was collared and trying to link forwards and three-quarters.

Another discovery was G. C. Wade, an Australian who was recognized as a match-winner by all who saw him play and especially by all who tried to tackle him. In Vassall's words, 'He was prodigiously strong, very fast, a first-rate swerver and he had a shove off you did not forget in a hurry.' Vassall in fact had persuaded the England selectors to make room for Wade in the team against Wales by letting him replace a forward who had dropped out—thus England started playing three three-quarters instead of two. When Wade died in 1922, obituaries described him as 'the best three-quarter back we ever had in England'. As, by that time pundits had seen the likes of Stoddart, Lockwood, Poulton and Lowe, there must be a case for including Wade amongst the all-time greats. At any rate he scored seven tries in his eight internationals and was always on the winning side.

Nine Oxford men played for England this season—including Scots, there were twelve internationals in residence plus four more who were later capped—and it is no wonder that the Varsity were unbeaten for over three years. From 1881 to 1885 they won 50 out of 56 games and drew the other 6. In 1884 they even defeated Yorkshire (unbeaten for three years) in a challenge match at Iffley Road.

It was not quite all Oxford, however, and Cambridge played its part in England's team. The wonderful Gurdon brothers, who had 'worn light Blue coats' from 1874 to 1877, were still as proficient in this third phase of rugger as they had been in the first two. J. H. Payne, a Cambridge Blue in 1879, played with great judgment, and indeed a pass from him in the North *v.* South trial of 1881 was the first recorded instance of a half putting a three-quarter away in a big match. There was also the remarkable H. G. Fuller who won six Cambridge Blues between 1878 and 1883 and led to fifth-year men being excluded from the Varsity match between 1886 and 1972. Fuller's bald pate was so conspicuous in the scrums that he is reputed to have invented the scrum cap!

Nor should Blackheath's W. N. 'Baby' Bolton, Wade's great rival as the best three-quarter of the day, be forgotten. He was reckoned to be faster than Wade ('for all his thirteen stone he could do the quarter-mile inside a minute') but made more mistakes.

England again won the Triple Crown in 1884 when they had basically the same side, the only new regular being C. J. B. Marriott, the Cambridge captain, a burly forward who was to become Secretary of the Rugby Football Union from 1907 to 1924.

Wales were met on the ground of the Leeds St John's Club, soon to be known as Leeds. Wade, Rotherham and Twynam scored tries for England, Bolton converting one. Wales replied with a converted try.

Once again a weak side went to Dublin—only seven men played in all three matches. In those days the team crossed on a Saturday and played on the following Monday so time off must have been a real problem. Payne made an opening for Bolton who finished up a fine run with a try. C. H. Sample, the Cambridge full back, kicked the ball over the bar and this was the only score of the match.

The first international at Rectory Field, Blackheath, attracted 8,000 spectators and Scotland were leading by a try to nil when R. S. Kindersley ran in and grounded the ball between the posts. There followed a delay of nearly ten minutes, the Scots claiming that they had earlier knocked the ball back and that there should have been a scrum down. The English claimed that a side should not profit from its own mistake (there was no such thing as advantage then), that knocking back was legal anyway and that, as England had not appealed (appeals were still essential), subsequent play was legal. When play was ultimately resumed, Bolton converted to give England a narrow victory although Scotland did not recognize it until 1886.

For the dispute had repercussions which lasted for six years! The R.F.U. cancelled fixtures with Scotland for 1885 because Scotland had not accepted the referee's decision. In 1886 Scotland accepted the 1884 result but denied the R.F.U.'s right to be sole law-makers and demanded an International Board. However England refused to serve on a board on which they only had equal voting powers with other countries. This led to Scotland, Ireland and Wales all refusing to play England in 1888 and 1889 and it was 1890 before internationals were resumed normally.

Thus the 1885 season was shorn of its biggest attraction—the Calcutta Cup match. At Swansea England won handsomely by one goal, four tries to one goal, one try, Wade running and dodging as he liked, and at Manchester Bolton decided the Irish match with a typical try when the scores were equal.

Bradford (founded 1866) had supplied H. W. T. Garnett, an interesting forward, 'always conspicuous on the field as playing barelegged without stockings or shinguards, having whilst a schoolboy learnt to despise the hack', to the first England XV against Scotland back in 1877, but they were now established as one of the premier clubs in England and contributed a succession of outstanding players.

The first was J. J. Hawcridge, a three-quarter with a stealthy stride and marvellous swerve who was styled the 'Artful Dodger'. He scored thirty-eight tries for Bradford in 1884–5 and, as a result of helping his side draw with the star-studded Oxford team, played in both England's internationals and ran in a try in each. These were his only caps as it was Hawcridge's ill luck to coincide with a glut of class threes.

Amongst them was his Bradford club mate Rawson Robertshaw, who in 1886 revolutionized England back play by introducing the concept of a centre three-quarter playing not for himself, like previous threes, but primarily to his wings. F. Bonsor, the Bradford half, was introduced into the England XV as Rotherham's partner in 1886: he always grassed his man and was a most dangerous attacking player; his feeding of the backs was of the highest order and he became the first Yorkshireman to captain his country. A third Bradford player to make the 1886 England side was E. Wilkinson, a brilliant forward in the open who scored tries in his first two internationals.

At Blackheath, Wales were winning by one goal to two tries when C. Elliott (Sunderland) caught the ball from a Welsh miskick and had a clear run-in. To the astonishment of everyone he made a mark. Up to 1921 any player on the side could take the kick after a mark and A. E. Stoddart (Blackheath) landed the goal which enabled England to win as both sides had a goal to their credit but England also had two tries.

Stoddart was one of England's great all-round sportsmen. He was one of the first 'flying wing' three-quarters, now that three-quarters were specialized. He emulated Hornby in captaining England at both rugger and cricket. He played in ten internationals and sixteen Tests and is the only man who has missed rugby caps because he spent winters cricketing abroad and cricket caps because he was on an overseas Rugby tour!

The Dublin match was won by a try to nil only, but that try typifies the way England was playing its rugby. Bonsor stole away from a scrum on the half-way line and passed to Robertshaw who ran right up to the Irish full back. Wilkinson was handy to touch down.

The Scottish fixture, restored temporarily, was a tough draw and brought to an end England's wonderful run of ten successive wins. It also marked the last appearance of Temple Gurdon, who had gathered an invincible team together at Richmond, including ex-Varsity stars such as Tristram, Wade and Rotherham and England forwards W. G. Clibborn and J. H. Dewhurst. Temple Gurdon captained England nine times and this draw was the only match England did not win under his leadership.

Rotherham was England's captain in 1887. Wade had returned to Australia to be 'capped' by New South Wales against Queensland and the British touring team in 1888, and was replaced by R. E. Lockwood, a fine wing three-quarter, always turning up at the right time in defence or attack, and an accurate place-kicker. Lockwood's club was Dewsbury, one of several northern places which were now coming into prominence although, to the annoyance of southerners, they could not be found in Bradshaw!

England's performances were disappointing. At Llanelly, on a skating rink, Wales held them to a draw for the first time. Ireland beat England for the first time and thus ended what is still England's record run of twelve games without defeat. They were so determined to win that one of their players, who had already had his holidays, got married the morning of the match to get off business. The Scottish match was drawn, defeat being averted only by a magnificent tackle by H. B. Tristram, the English full back, who stopped the famous Scottish heavyweight three-quarter W. E. MacLagan in full stride on the goal-line.

The game was played in fog, a suitable curtain because England's rugby was about to enter a period of disruption.

Chapter Four

The First Tours 1888–92

As recounted in the previous chapter, England was boycotted by the home countries in 1888 and 1889. However, England actually chose a team and awarded caps in 1888 although they had no one to play!

As compensation for the lack of big fixtures, England held two North *v.* South trial matches. Scoring by points had been introduced in 1887 with all goals counting three points and a try one, and the first trial was drawn 1–1. However, Somerset had beaten Gloucestershire 10–0, Devon 24–0 and even Yorkshire, and as Sam Woods said, 'The papers discovered that we could play down west.' Seven Somerset men were in the South XV who defeated the North 4–3 in the return, and as a result two were selected for 'England'. One was F. H. Fox, a half-back from Wellington who 'always seemed able to obtain possession of the ball'. The other was P. Froude Hancock, one of five brothers who played for Wiveliscombe and Somerset. Froude, a forward whose height and weight made him useful in the lines-out, had already been capped in 1886: it was said that he was always in good condition because he hunted stags and followed beagles. One of the Hancock brothers, Frank, moved to Cardiff where he originated the four three-quarters game and actually captained Wales when they first used four three-quarters in 1886. As Scotland beat them they abandoned the experiment for two years.

Eight of the 1888 'team' had already played for England and five did subsequently, but Percy Robertshaw (Bradford, brother of Rawson) and H. Eagles (Salford) were awarded England caps without ever turning out for their country.

Eagles had the consolation of being included in the first British side to tour overseas. The tour, to Australasia, was run by two cricket professionals, Alfred Shaw and Arthur Shrewsbury, who had already managed successful, and profitable, cricket tours there, and was regarded with suspicion by the R.F.U. The party were away for ten months and the day before they sailed in March 1888 Clowes of Halifax was declared a professional for accepting £15 for a football outfit. It was too late to check on the others, the majority of whom came from North of England clubs like Swinton, Batley, Dewsbury and Rochdale Hornets, and, when they returned, affidavits from the players that they had gained no pecuniary benefit from the tour were accepted.

The tour captain was R. L. Seddon, a forward who had been capped by England from Broughton Rangers in 1887, but he was drowned sculling in Australia and A. E. Stoddart, the vice-captain, took over. Stoddart had been cricketing in Australia in 1887–8 and stayed behind to await the footballers. In Australia the tourists played sixteen games under Rugby laws, winning fourteen and drawing two. They also undertook eighteen matches under Victorian rules—to the embarrassment of the R.F.U. In New Zealand they won thirteen, drew four and lost two. The British team took their own umpires,' who allowed heeling back, and New Zealand rugby soon imitated them in disregarding the offside rule as regards forwards in the scrum and in using the rear of the scrum as the starting point of the passing game. In his speech after New Zealand had thrashed England in 1905, the manager of the first All Blacks, G. H. Dixon, acknowledged that 'New Zealand owed all the development of the game to the visit of the 1888 team'.

Despite the boycott, England did play an international in 1889—against the 'New Zealand Native Football Representatives'. This, the first colonial side to visit Britain, was popularly, because it was confined to men born in New Zealand, but inaccurately, because it included four whites, known as the 'Maoris'. It had played in New Zealand and Australia before arriving in England and on its return played in those countries again, completing 107 matches before it dispersed!

To cover expenses in Britain they undertook seventy-four matches in twenty-five weeks, the majority of them in the north of England where the 'brass' was.

When they came to Blackheath to play England, they had

beaten Ireland 13–4 in Dublin and lost to Wales 0–5 at Swansea. Over 10,000 turned up, curious to see these tourists who performed a war dance ('Haka') before the kick-off. The teams were:

England: A. Royle (Broughton Rangers); R. E. Lockwood (Dewsbury), J. W. Sutcliffe (Heckmondwike), A. E. Stoddart (Blackheath); F. Bonsor (Bradford), W. M. Scott (Cambridge University); C. Anderton (Manchester Free Wanderers), H. Bedford (Morley), J. W. Cave (Cambridge University), F. Evershed (Burton), D. Jowett (Heckmondwike), F. W. Lowrie (Wakefield Trinity), A. Robinson (Blackheath), H. Wilkinson (Halifax), W. Yiend (Hartlepool Rovers).

New Zealand Native Team: W. Warbrick; C. Madigan, W. Wynyard, E. M'Causland; P. Keogh, D. Gage, W. Elliott; R. Taiaroa, H. Lee, G. Williams, W. Anderson, R. Maynard, G. Wynyard, J. Ellison, D. Stewart.

Bedford, a heavy, dashing forward, scored two tries in the first half, Stoddart got in after a magnificent run, Evershed scored in the corner and Sutcliffe converted and the last-named also went over for a try to give England victory by 7 points to 0.

Evershed's try was disputed and three of the visitors temporarily left the field, to the annoyance of referee Rowland Hill who, as Hon. Secretary of the R.F.U., had arranged their fixtures.

This was Sutcliffe's only Rugby international. His long and accurate drops and punts into touch had set a new fashion which helped make Yorkshire invincible—their forwards, instead of running back to help the backs, waited for Sutcliffe to return the ball up field. It was Yorkshire who inflicted on the Maoris their heaviest defeat—16–4 at Wakefield. The Football Association had legitimized professionalism in 1885 (with the immediate result that no more amateur clubs won the F.A. Cup) and Sutcliffe's kicking powers attracted the attention of Football League clubs. He decided to turn to the only code where he could legally earn money, signed for Bolton Wanderers and kept goal for England five times, thus following R. H. Birkett and C. P. Wilson as a dual rugger and soccer English international.

Evershed was the first man to play for England from the Midland Counties Union since it had been founded ten years before. He came from Burton, founded in 1870 and the oldest club in the Midlands, and his selection was facilitated by a decision to transfer the Midlands from the North (where Midlanders had been squeezed out by Yorkshire and Lancashire players) to the South for trial purposes. Evershed, who attained full speed in an instant, had a peculiar stride that disguised his pace and a quick swerve. He was criticized as not being a scrummager but did more work in the pack than he was given credit for and was unrivalled as a try-scoring forward.

Another interesting debutant against the Maoris was Martin Scott (not to be confused with his brother Mason Scott, also a Cambridge, Northumberland and England half-back). He was one of the first men to specialize in selling the dummy and 'made the Maoris look like a lot of kids'.

This England team was regarded as exceedingly strong and it came as a great shock when they resumed fixtures with the home countries in 1890 that at Dewsbury Wales, at their seventh attempt, gained their first victory over England. W. H. Stadden, the Cardiff half, tricked his opposing number by bounding the ball out of touch (a practice that was abolished in 1905) and dodged over for the only score of the match. This so impressed the locals that ere long Stadden was playing for Dewsbury!

To raise funds in the absence of internationals the R.F.U. had established a Champion County *v.* The Rest of England game in 1889. There was no County Championship until 1891 so the R.F.U. examined the counties' records and declared the county with the best record Champions. As Yorkshire were undefeated in 1889 and 1890 there was no problem who was to play the Rest these years, and, between the Welsh match and the Scottish, Yorkshire had the temerity to defeat the Rest 6–4.

As a result, there were wholesale changes for the Calcutta Cup match in Edinburgh. J. Dyson, a sprinter from Huddersfield, was brought on to the wing and J. Toothill (Bradford), E. Holmes (Manningham), D. Jowett (Heckmondwike) and H. Bedford (Morley) joined J. L. Hickson (Bradford) in the pack. There should have been seven Yorkshire players in the England team but Bonsor, the famous half, 'begged off under notice' to captain his club in a Yorkshire cup-tie. He was never picked for England again and those worried about the purity of the game in North England had more ammunition.

However, the remaining Tykes did their stuff, especially their five forwards who showed the form that had made the 'Yorkshire rush' proverbial. Fox, the first West Countryman to captain England, played like the little wonder he was at half-back and Evershed and Dyson scored tries, Jowett converting one. Pending the decision of the International Board, international matches in 1890 were decided under the rules of the home country, and, according to the Scottish method of scoring, England won 6–0. Thus the defeat of England by Yorkshire led to the defeat of Scotland by England!

This year the Irish match was the last of the season and at Blackheath England won 3–0 and so shared the international championship with Scotland, each country having two wins and one defeat.

In addition to Evershed and Hickson, already mentioned, only W. G. Mitchell, Richmond's full-back, P. H. Morrison, a Cambridge wing, and three forwards—A. Robinson (Blackheath), J. H. Rogers (Moseley) and S. M. J. Woods (Cambridge)—played in all three internationals.

The vigorous Rogers was the first cap from the Moseley Club, which had been formed in 1873, and in the last game of the 1885–6 season had created a sensation by beating Cardiff, all set to celebrate the unbeaten season that has still eluded them.

Woods, who played cricket for both Australia and England, seemed to dominate every game in which he played. It appeared impossible for any opponent to escape the clutch of his huge hands and he was an awe-inspiring figure dribbling downfield.

Against Scotland another Cambridge Blue, R. L. Aston, played as fine a centre game as ever seen. Aston only played for England twice but in 1891 he created a lasting impression with the first British team to visit South Africa, scoring thirty tries.

In 1891 England were captained by a debutant, F. H. R. Alderson, a scientific centre who over the Christmas of 1890 had played for Hartlepool Rovers against the Barbarians in the famous wandering club's first match and for them against Bradford in their second. Before the week was out he was leading England to a 7–3 victory over Wales at Newport.

Alderson, a Cambridge Blue in 1887 and 1888, converted two of England's tries which were scored by wing P. Christopherson (2) and forward R. D. Budworth, both of Blackheath.

This season had seen the start of a county championship competition with fifteen counties placed in four groups, the winners of each group going forward to a second series and playing each other. The side to top this table were champions and the first champions were Lancashire. Five of their players played in the season's internationals—J. Berry (half), T. Kent and R. P. Wilson (forwards) for England, and the other two, having left Swansea for Oldham, for Wales! This season also marked the first appearance for England of a man direct from the Harlequins—W. R. M. Leake, a half-back. Hitherto men like A. E. Stoddart and G. L. Jeffrey who had started with the 'Quins had moved on to Blackheath to win their caps.

In Dublin, Lockwood, recalled to international championship matches after four years' absence, proved that he was still the best wing in Britain with two tries and two conversions in England's 9–0 victory, and England looked all set for the Triple Crown, especially as Scotland had to travel to Richmond. However the crowd of 15,000 saw England badly beaten 9–3. Contemporary comment was caustic: 'The English fifteen were certainly the most disappointing that ever represented this country.' The forwards 'were hustled and routed, and there was not an ounce of scrummage work amongst the nine of them while it is no exaggeration to say that in the second half they literally chucked it.'

In 1891 the R.F.U. got together a team to visit South Africa, where a Rugby Board had been formed two years previously. The captain was W. E. MacLagen, one of four Scottish internationals to make the tour. Four of the tourists had won England caps. The hard tackling W. G. Mitchell had been England's full-back in all six internationals since England had re-entered the championship; W. E. Bromet, of Tadcaster and Yorkshire, a perfect forward—untiring in the scrum and fast as a three-quarter in the open—had been capped against Wales and Ireland in 1891 and had had the good fortune to be injured for the Scottish débâcle, and R. L. Aston and P. F. Hancock had played for England in 1890. Two more of the party—Arthur Rotherham (a cousin of Alan) and H. Marshall, both halves—were subsequently capped.

They won all nineteen matches including four Tests, the first ever played by South Africa, and were the last touring side to leave South Africa unbeaten until England in 1972.

Only three men who played in the 1891 Calcutta Cup match played in England's first match of the 1892 campaign—against Wales at Rectory Field, Blackheath. Wales, captained by the great A. J. Gould from centre, included W. J. Bancroft, with 33 their most capped full back until J. P. R. Williams, but England won 17–0. (Goals from tries had been upgraded to five points and unconverted tries to two, with the penalty goal three points and other goals four.) England's forwards showed passing that would be a credit to three-quarters—two of them, W. Nichol (Brighouse Rangers) and the inevitable Evershed, scoring tries. G. C. Hubbard, a Blackheath wing, and Alderson, again captain, also crossed, Lockwood converting two tries and Alderson one. There was no attempt to convert the other try because the Welshmen claimed that in bringing the ball out for the conversion two Englishmen had handled it—as the law then stood only the placer could bring it out. On their appeal no kick at goal was allowed.

For the Irish match at Manchester, England included J. Marsh, a Swinton centre who in 1889, while at Edinburgh University, had played twice for Scotland. Ireland were beaten 7–0, Evershed and L. J. Percival, an Oxford forward, scoring tries, Woods converting one, and England went to Edinburgh with the Triple Crown at stake.

The game was a close one and described as more like a cup-tie than an international, 'the brandy bottle having frequently to be requisitioned for the knocked-out ones'. It was Woods's policy that when forwards lost the ball they should break up at once and join in the defence. Indeed, he had ensured that a forward who had held on to him in the scrum in the Irish match never played for England again. England's defence was so good in 1892 that they did not concede a single point, and to this day they remain the only side to have won the Triple Crown with no points against.

Woods himself followed up a kick by Alderson and scored a try which Lockwood converted to bring England victory by 5 points to nil.

England ended the season with this team:

J. Coop (Leigh); R. E. Lockwood (Heckmondwike), F. H. R. Alderson (Hartlepool Rovers), J. Dyson (Huddersfield); A. Briggs (Bradford), H. Varley (Liversedge); J. Toothill (Bradford), W. Nichol (Brighouse), W. E. Bromet (Tadcaster), H. Bradshaw (Bramley), F. Evershed (Burton), E. Bullogh (Wigan), W. Yiend (Hartlepool Rovers), T. Kent (Salford), S. M. J. Woods (Somerset).

Eight from Yorkshire, three from Lancashire, two from Durham, one from Midland Counties, one from Somerset and none from London. There was no doubt where the power of English Rugby then lay. But this power was soon to be lost to the Union game, with disastrous consequences for England's Rugby.

In fact it was to be twenty-one years before England won the Triple Crown again.

Chapter Five

Flattering to Deceive 1893–6

The 'no points against' Triple Crown of 1892 did not presage a golden era, though for the next four seasons England were in with a chance of the championship and their performances were a pleasant memory in the dark age that was to follow.

The year 1893 opened with an unexpected defeat in one of the most remarkable matches in international history.

Stoddart, back from Australia, was made England's captain and only seven of the men who had earned immortality the previous season were retained for the visit to Cardiff. Politics appear to have influenced selection and the blunt reporting of the day stated that the southern players lost England the game because they had taken no trouble to keep in training during the Christmas festivities and long frost that had preceded the match. In fact it was a miracle that the Cardiff pitch was playable. Five hundred nightwatchmen's braziers were kept burning day and night and used up eighteen tons of coal to thaw out the ground.

F. C. Lohden, a Blackheath forward, put England 2 points up with a try. H. Marshall, one of two Blackheath halves playing, scored two tries, one converted by Stoddart, to give England what should have been an unassailable 9–0 lead. But England faded badly. Wales had reverted to the four three-quarter system, and the extra man led to two tries, one converted, to reduce the deficit to two points. A brief England rally saw Marshall, 'a marvel of quickness and brilliance', score his third try—an amazing feat for a man in his first and, because of injury, only international. The great Welsh centre A. J. Gould touched down for his second try to make the score 11–9. Since 1892 penalty kicks for goal had been allowed in internationals, and, when England were penalized near the touch line, Gould instructed Bancroft to try a place kick. However, Bancroft did not want to risk having a man to place the ball for him as the laws required up to 1925, and insisted on dropping for goal. Gould threw the ball down in disgust and, while he was walking away, Bancroft snatched a dramatic win by one goal, two tries, one penalty (12 points) to one goal, three tries (11).

But this is not the end of the story. The Welsh Union were allowing three points for a try in their internal matches and many spectators left the ground thinking that Bancroft's kick had levelled the scores 14–14. But the International Board did not sanction the three-point try until the following season. Thus, by one point, Wales, having lost all three games the previous year, took the first step towards its first Triple Crown!

The Irish match in Dublin was a series of forward rushes in which the heavy England forwards had slight superiority—one of them, the burly H. Bradshaw of Bramley, scoring an early try, leaving a trail of bruised men en route, and E. W. Taylor slipping round the scrum for another to give England a 4–0 victory. 'Little Billy' Taylor (Rockliff and Northumberland) won fourteen caps between 1892 and 1899 and captained England: fast, dodgy, a clever kicker and a good tackler, he was described as 'the prince of half-backs'.

However, at Leeds the English pack was pushed around by the Scots and, though Scotland could not cross England's line, they dropped two goals, one by the veteran forward Boswell who 'made a habit of such things'.

In many respects, 1893–4 marks the start of modern Rugby football. Referees were permitted to blow the whistle whenever the laws were broken, without appeal; the 'Advantage Law' was introduced; the three-point try became universal—and England bowed to the inevitable by fielding four three-quarters.

For the record, England's first four-man three-quarter line was S. Morfitt (West Hartlepool), C. A. Hooper (Middlesex Wanderers), R. E. Lockwood (Heckmondwike), F. Firth (Halifax). Three of them were new caps and there were seven newcomers in the England team 'of unknown quality' that started the season with a surprisingly large win (24–3) over the previous year's champions—Wales. The match was played at Birkenhead Park and was in fact the second international staged on the ground as back in 1887 Wales had received Ireland there to save the Irish Union travelling expenses.

England's forwards frequently rushed the Welsh in the loose. Morfitt, a determined, fast wing, scored a try after a long run by C. M. Wells (Harlequins). Wells, rated as England's best swerver to date, was in the habit of standing back in 'Quins matches in their opponents' 25 and receiving the ball from his fellow half who worked the scrum alone. Another decade was to elapse before England allowed this revolutionary practice and in internationals Wells had to stand by the scrum with his partner—this time E. W. Taylor. Taylor kicked a goal from a mark made by Hooper (worth 4 points up to 1905). The relentless Bradshaw forced through for England's second try, Lockwood scored England's third and Taylor their fourth, all being converted.

England's new full-back, J. F. Byrne (Moseley), outshone the great Bancroft on the day. Byrne remained first choice for five years and won a reputation as the ideal orthodox full-back—safe hands, invariably where the ball came, a quick and long punter and rock-like in defence. He was also an excellent place-kicker capable of landing goals from half-way and in 1896, as the only current English international to tour South Africa with the last British side to win a Test series there for 78 years, scored 127 points. Until 1960 Byrne remained the only player to have topped 100 points on a tour of South Africa and the only tourists to have exceeded his 127 there have been the All Blacks D. B. Clarke (175 in 1960), W. F. McCormick (132 in 1970) and L. W. Mains (132 in 1976), and the Lion A. R. Irvine (156 in 1974).

But to return to 1894. England's fine start was not maintained and at Blackheath Ireland won 7–5, a last minute dropped goal regaining the lead for Ireland after Taylor's conversion of a try by the 'Little Marvel', Lockwood, playing in his last international, had seemingly won the game for England. Ireland went on to its first Triple Crown.

The selectors retained faith in a losing side against press advice and Scotland won by two tries to nil.

Selection committees were conservative at this time and the following season, 1895, only seventeen players were called on—a 'low' not equalled until 1924. One of the changes was forced on them when Byrne was injured for the Welsh match. Of the 'ever-presents' six, including three Varsity men, played for Blackheath in 1895.

Three of the three-quarters—J. H. C. Fegan (Blackheath), E. M. Baker (Oxford University) and W. B. Thomson (Blackheath)—and both halves—R. H. Cattell (Moseley) and E. W. Taylor (Rockliff)—appeared in all three matches.

So, wonderful to relate, did the same pack—G. M. Carey, F. O. Poole (both Oxford University), F. Mitchell, W. E. Tucker (both Cambridge University), C. Thomas (Devon), H. W. Finlinson (Blackheath), W. E. Bromet (Richmond) and S. M. J. Woods (Somerset), the captain and pack leader, in his last season at the age of twenty-six. This was still the day of the all-round forward—skilled at scrummaging, as useful with the feet as a soccer player, sound at tackling and with safe hands for catching in the line-out or in the open field—and as late as 1945 there were still those who swore that this was the greatest England pack of all time.

The season opened with a brilliant 14–6 victory over Wales at Swansea—England's last win in the principality for eighteen years. The Oxford centres F. A. Leslie-Jones and Baker outclassed Gould, the Welsh captain. Thomson, Leslie-Jones, Carey and Woods scored tries. Mitchell, who later played Test cricket for both England and South Africa, converted one.

The Irish match at Dublin was played on a swamp, and won by two tries to one. It was recorded that, 'realizing the futility of trying to handle, the famous English pack settled down to genuine scrummage work and their superiority was manifest'.

The Calcutta Cup match at Richmond was also for the Triple Crown and there was bitter disappointment that England lost 3–6—a result that must cast doubt on the greatness of the 1895 side. J. F. Byrne had the distinction of kicking the first penalty goal in England's history!

Next season, 1896, was the last year until 1907 that England opened their campaign with a win and were thus, albeit fleetingly, in with a chance of winning the (four countries) championship—to lose one of only three matches virtually put paid to aspirations.

At Blackheath England beat Wales 25–0, still their biggest victory over the Welsh since points were introduced in 1888. The team to gain this historic victory was:

S. Houghton (Cheshire); S. Morfitt (Yorkshire), J. Valentine (Lancashire), E. M. Baker (Oxford), E. F. Fookes (Yorkshire); R. H. Cattell (Blackheath), E. W. Taylor (Northumberland); A. Starks, J. W. Ward, W. Whiteley, T. J. Rhodes (all Yorkshire), J. Pinch (Lancashire), L. F. Giblin (Cambridge), F. Mitchell, G. M. Carey (both Blackheath).

(It is an interesting sidelight on the development of England's rugby that at this time players were listed by their counties if from the North or South-west, where the County Championship was, and still is, regarded as pre-eminent; and by their clubs if from London, Oxford or Cambridge.)

Valentine, capped after a gap of six years and barred after 1896 because his club (Swinton) joined the Northern Union, put Morfitt over. Cattell, a half-back noted for his weight and strength, went over for two tries, Mitchell got through the Welsh forwards for a try that Valentine converted, and Fookes, 'twelve stone of bone and muscle from Sowerby Bridge', scored near the corner to make the half-time score 17–0. After the interval Morfitt jumped and dodged through the thick of the opposition and ran thirty yards for his second try and Taylor made the opening for Fookes to cross again. Taylor's conversion made the score 25–0.

But this was in the nature of a last gesture by England who lost 4–10 to Ireland at the West Riding Club, Leeds (a 40-yard dropped goal by Byrne) and 0–11 to Scotland at Hampden Park, Glasgow, where England were 'a long way second best in the rough play'. In fact England had embarked on a lean spell and the reason for the abrupt change in fortunes is not hard to find. In August 1895, eleven Yorkshire Clubs (Batley, Bradford, Brighouse Rangers, Halifax, Huddersfield, Hull, Hunslet, Leeds, Liversedge, Manningham, Wakefield Trinity) and nine Lancashire (Broughton Rangers, Leigh, Oldham, Rochdale Hornets, St Helens, Tyldesley, Warrington, Widnes and Wigan) formed the Northern Union (known since 1922 as the Rugby League) over the question of broken-time payments. Before long other clubs such as Runcorn, Dewsbury, Salford, York, Barrow, Hull K. R. and Bramley joined them.

The number of Yorkshire clubs in membership of the R.F.U. dwindled from 150 to 14. As England's largest county, Yorkshire should have dominated the County Championship and provided a big share of England's teams as their cricketers did. But, having won the Championship five years running from 1892 to 1896 (including the first with group winners engaging in a knock-out), they did not win it again until 1926. Lancashire, another populous county, who were champions in 1891, did not repeat the feat until 1935.

It is customary to think of other countries, especially Wales, being drained of outstanding players by the Rugby League, but in fact Rugby Union stars rarely make the grade at international level at the thirteen-a-side game. British Rugby League teams are dominated by North Countrymen who have played little if any Rugby Union. The loss to English Rugby Union as a result of the split is incalculable.

Chapter Six

Lean Years 1897–1905

There followed nine seasons during which, of 27 games, only 6 were won, 3 drawn and 18 lost. Although there were only three matches a season, England called on an average of 25 men each campaign, with a record 31 in 1899.

It is difficult to find anything encouraging except the rare win and the odd individual performance.

England played the other Home Countries in 1897 but there was no international championship because Scotland and Ireland refused to play Wales. At Newport A. J. Gould captained Wales to an 11–0 win over England in his twenty-seventh and what proved to be his last international. Present in the crowd was W. E. MacLagen who, with twenty-five games for Scotland between 1878 and 1890, had been the previous record holder. To mark Gould's achievement, he was presented with a house by admirers and the Scottish and Irish Unions, regarding this as a breach of the laws concerning professionalism, broke off relations with Wales.

England lost to Ireland in Dublin 9–13, Byrne kicking two penalties, one from half-way, the other from touch; but at Manchester Athletic Ground, Fallowfield, there was an unexpected 12–3 victory over the Scots, who were reputed to have left the Calcutta Cup in Edinburgh!

The English centres—Richmond's W. L. Bunting, who this season helped Kent become the first southern county to win the championship, and O. G. Mackie, who was still at Cambridge although he had toured South Africa in 1896—gave plenty of chances to their wings E. F. Fookes (Sowerby Bridge and Yorkshire) and G. C. Robinson (Percy Park and Northumberland). After a scoreless first half, Fookes got over in the corner and Byrne converted. The nippy 'Tot' Robinson, first in a line of Northumberland wingers who represented England, also scored and Byrne dropped a goal. The Scottish forwards gave way to the hard shoving and fine footwork of the English pack, who for the first time for thirteen years included no Yorkshiremen but had two typical forwards from Cumberland, runners up in the county championship, E. Knowles (Millom) and James Davidson (Aspatria), plus R. F. Oakes (Hartlepool Rovers and Durham) who was to become a leading administrator and staunch upholder of pure amateurism. This season too saw the debut of F. M. Stout (Gloucester and Richmond), a forward who played forty-four times for Gloucestershire and fourteen for England. As a former association footballer, his dribbling was superb and he was the only man to go on both the first official British tour to Australia in 1899 (when three tests were won and one lost) and the third British tour to South Africa in 1903 (when two tests were drawn and the third lost).

In 1898 England opened with a defeat by Ireland, who won 9–6 thanks to a late try by their great half Louis Magee.

At Powderhall Grounds, more associated with running and cycling than rugger, P. M. R. Royds, a Blackheath and Kent three-quarter, later known as an expert on the Laws, charged down a kick and got a try, but Scotland equalized and the match was drawn 3–3. It is interesting to recall that the R.U. party from London travelled from King's Cross by the east coast route the day before the match, with the Devon, Midland and Northumberland representatives going separately, and it was decided not to hold a team meeting the morning of the match.

Scotland still refused to play Wales owing to the Gould dispute, and England did not meet them until the last match of the season by which time Gould himself had diplomatically retired from international football. At Blackheath England won 14–7, their last victory over Wales for twelve years. Fookes, a winger who took a lot of stopping and had an excellent defence, scored two tries and the brothers Frank and Percy Stout one each, Byrne (the captain) making one conversion.

The year 1899 was aptly described as 'a season of unrelieved disaster'. Not only did England lose all three games but they scored only three points—a try by Robinson versus Wales at Swansea.

However, this was lost sight of in the score, 26–3 to Wales, who had been beaten in the last match of the previous season. W. M. Llewellyn scored four tries, a number that has not been exceeded for Wales, and it was described as the 'most surprising result in the history of Rugby football'. Reports bluntly named three England players as not worth their places. Only three men—P. W. Stout, a useful centre, Arthur Rotherham, a 'heroic' half-back, and H. W. Dudgeon, 'England's premier forward' (all from Richmond)—held their places throughout the season, which finished with defeats from Ireland (6–0) and Scotland (5–0).

Most interesting of the new men tried was H. T. Gamlin, a twenty-year-old, 6 foot, 14 stone full-back from Wellington who had been playing for Somerset since he was sixteen. His style of play was unorthodox but remarkably effective. He fielded the ball in his two hands instead of using his chest to make a cradle, while he did not believe in tackling low but used his octopus-like grip to envelop man and ball and stop a pass. It was said of him that he did not tackle a man—he crushed him. He certainly had plenty of practice as the fifteen England teams he played behind won only four games.

Northumberland had won the county championship in 1898 and were runners-up the following year, and (as well as Robinson) G. R. Gibson, E. W. Taylor and S. Anderson were capped by England in 1899. Devon's success in winning its first championship in 1899 was reflected in the selection of J. C. Matters, a big dashing centre from R.N.E.C. Keyham who was lost to the game early by overseas posting, and the recall of Barnstaple's C. Thomas, while in 1900 S. F. Coopper, also R.N.E.C., a winger renowned for hurdling full backs and kicking over his own head, gained the first of his caps. Coopper was R.F.U. Secretary from 1924 to 1947.

Next year, 1900, opened with the only full international at Gloucester where 15,000 saw Wales win 13–3 and start their 'Golden Era'.

However, at Richmond England won their first game for two years by beating Ireland 15–4. John Daniell made his name in this, his first international as captain. Daniell was a member of the 1899 Cambridge pack, all eight of whom were, or became, internationals, and laid the foundations of their 22–0 win over Oxford, but injury prevented his playing regularly for England and he won only seven caps. However, J. E. Raphael, who played under him, wrote, 'At his best he was in a class by himself if only by reason of his incomparable knowledge of the forward game as it should be played and his wonderful capacity for making eight forwards who were absolute strangers to one another before going on the field play together as if they had played side by side all their lives.' Daniell later earned a reputation as an England selector at both Rugby and cricket.

Scotland, met at Inverleith because the old Edinburgh Academy ground at Raeburn Place was, with its temporary stands, proving too expensive, were held to a 0–0 draw before a record 30,000 crowd. The only men to play in all three internationals were G. Gordon Smith, a Blackheath and Kent centre who had played for Cornwall while at Camborne School of Mines, G. H. Marsden, a half from Morley and Yorkshire, R. W. Bell, a Cambridge forward, and J. 'Bim' Baxter, a Cheshire forward who put Birkenhead Park (founded 1871) on the map and won a bronze medal for yachting in the 1908 Olympics. Against Wales J. W. Jarman became the first cap from Bristol, formed in 1888 by the amalgamation of two local clubs.

In 1901 England again lost all three games. Daniell, the chosen captain, did not play in any of the matches which resulted in victories for Wales at Cardiff (13–0), Ireland at Dublin (10–6) and Scotland at Blackheath (18–3). One frank report stated that England's weakness was outside the scrummage and they had 'no halves or three-quarters', which was somewhat hard on Robinson, who against Scotland in his eighth and last international scored his eighth try—and for the fifth time scored England's only try in a game.

Devon, who won the championship in 1901, supplied E. W. Roberts and A. O'Neill to the pack: both were masters of the art of dribbling; it was said that Roberts, who was also a noted exponent of the wheel, never struck the ball with his foot but always with his shins! E. W. Elliott, a Sunderland and Durham wing, was the only back to play in all three matches. Forwards to keep their places all through were H. Alexander, Birkenhead Park, and N. C. Fletcher, Old Merchant Taylors, while against Scotland H. Weston put 'Northampton and East Midlands' into the England record books, East Midlands being in only their fourth season as an independent county.

As champion county of 1900–1, Devon played the Rest of England at Exeter in 1901–2 and won 8–0. As a result, six of their men—P. L. Nicholas and S. F. Coopper (wings) and D. Dobson, L. R. Tosswill, S. G. Williams and J. Willcocks (forwards)—played against Wales at Blackheath, and, although England lost, the 'yearning for the West Country after much neglect' was described as 'profitable'! Alexander led the pack in the absence of Daniell and they 'shoved hard and were for ever on the ball'. In fact England led by 8 points (tries by Dobson and J. J. Robinson, a Headingley forward previously capped while at Cambridge nine years before, one converted) to 6 when, five minutes from 'no side', B. Oughtred, who helped Durham win the championship in 1902, got offside when his opposite number Dicky Owen, the wily Welsh half, pretended to pick up from a scrum and Wales snatched a 9–8 victory with a dropped penalty.

The Irish match was before 20,000 at Leicester where T. H. Crumbie was developing a ground fit to be an international venue. England kept Oughtred, who had lost them the Welsh game, and he played wonderfully well. J. T. Taylor, a former Yorkshire captain who was playing for West Hartlepool and Durham, was England's hero behind with his superb tackling and kicking at centre; 'Long John' was regarded as the best drop-kicker in England though he never dropped a goal in any of his eleven internationals. After Ireland had equalized a try by Coopper, Daniell, back as captain, addressed a few terse sentences to his forwards and went down in the middle of the front row. Getting the ball and gripping firmly the men on either side of him, he went straight ahead and before the Irish realized it, England gained 25 yards by honest, straightforward shoving. From the line-out on the Irish line Williams scored the winning try.

At Inverleith England beat Scotland for the first time since 1897. Williams, the indefatigable Devon Albion forward, and Taylor gave England a 6–0 lead. Scotland scored a try but Gamlin played them on his own in the last quarter, when he kept them out with four tackles when all seemed lost.

Two wins out of three promised better things for 1903 but England were again whitewashed.

At Swansea Wales won 21–5. They lost their captain and winger T. W. Pearson after twenty-five minutes. J. Hodges was pulled out of the pack to replace him and scored three tries! Winger J. H. Miles became the first cap from Leicester, winners of the Midland Counties Cup every year from 1898 to 1905 when they withdrew to give other clubs a chance, and R. H. Spooner, a Lancashire centre, became the last man to represent England at both cricket and Rugby until M. J. K. Smith. They were amongst the many men who have been capped once for England against Wales and then made scapegoats for defeat.

At Dublin Ireland won 6–0 and at Richmond Scotland won 10–6 to take the Triple Crown. R. Forrest, a left wing from Somerset, dodged over for a try, Dobson scored from a forward rush, and the difference between the sides was only a dropped goal.

In 1904 England opened in promising fashion at Leicester with a 14–14 draw with Wales—the only time between 1898 and 1910 that England did not lose to the Celts. The Scottish referee penalized a Welsh half so much that he declined to put the ball in the scrum and handed it to one of the English pair—P. S. Hancock (Richmond) or W. V. Butcher (Bristol). Elliott scored two tries and A. T. Brettargh, a centre from Liverpool Old Boys and Lancashire, another, one being converted, and Gamlin, in his last season, landed a penalty. England led 14–10 when a Welshman made a mark and, as allowed up to 1921, gave the ball to the best kicker on the side—and Winfield dropped the goal to equalize. This was the last important match to be decided by a 4-point goal from a mark, as a year later its value was reduced to 3 points.

It was reckoned that England would have had an unassailable lead but for poor place kicking. The culprit was E. J. Vivyan from Devon Albion, who missed a conversion under the posts and four penalties. However, he came good in the next match when Ireland were beaten 19–0 at Blackheath. Vivyan was an eccentric genius who, in the opinion of J. E. Raphael, ought to have been one of the greatest three-quarters the world had seen. He had 'an almost inhuman capacity for leaving his swerve till the very last moment' and 'he could moreover make it pretty well at right angles when travelling at full speed', yet he lacked something. However, in the match in question, with two tries which he converted, he became the first man to score 10 points in a match for England (points had not been introduced when L. Stokes kicked his 6 goals against Wales in 1881). N. Moore, a Bristol and Somerset forward in his only international season, also scored two tries and T. Simpson, a side-stepping wing from Rockliff and Northumberland, one. The pack—J. Daniell (Richmond and Middlesex), B. A. Hill (Kent, county champions in 1904), F. M. Stout (Gloucestershire), P. F. Hardwick (Northumberland), N. Moore (Somerset), J. G. Milton (East Midlands), G. H. Keeton (Richmond) and C. J. Newbold (Cambridge) —was described as England's best for years.

Jumbo Milton, son of W. H. who had been capped in 1874–5 and brother of C. H., to be capped in 1906, played a full season while still at Bedford School. He was fully developed physically and technically at the age of eighteen but went to South Africa when twenty-two, having subsequently played for Camborne School of Mines and Cornwall.

As usual, the Scottish match at Inverleith was a forward battle. Vivyan equalized with a try but gave Scotland the winning try—and the championship—when he had a kick charged down.

In 1905 England lost all three matches for the fourth time in seven years. At Cardiff Wales scored seven tries and won 25–0, the only redeeming feature being the good work of F. C. Hulme, a right half from Birkenhead Park. Hulme had been a member of the British side that had toured Australia and New Zealand under Scotland's D. R. Bedell-Sivright in 1904. They had won all fourteen matches (including three Tests) in Australia but—a sign of things to come—had lost 9–3 to New Zealand in the first Test played between Britain and the All Blacks.

Ireland won 17–3 at Cork, the outstanding player being Basil Maclear, a centre born in Hampshire and educated at Bedford, but unwanted by England and selected by Ireland because he was stationed at Cork.

The dismal story continued at Richmond, when England lost their only home game of the season. In the days of three internationals England, in 'odd' years, had to play Wales and Ireland away before receiving Scotland at home. By the last match they were often demoralized, and it is no coincidence that they lost all three games in 1899, 1901 and 1903.

And 1905 was no exception to the pattern. Scotland won 8–0. J. E. Raphael (Oxford University and Old Merchant Taylors) received honourable mention in this match for his strong tackling and well judged touch kicking. A resourceful centre with a deceptive swerve, Raphael was rated by the great Welsh centre Gwyn Nicholls as a capable exponent of the four three-quarter game—praise indeed. Raphael incidentally captained the first R.F.U. team to tour the Argentine in 1910.

England had a new captain in 1905, V. H. Cartwright of Oxford University. 'Being always the best forward on the side he was invariably in the middle of the front row and the most likely to tackle the wing three-quarter.' It was said of him that when he wanted to wheel he nearly broke the necks of his opposing forwards swinging the scrum round. He had the ability to get something extra out of his men, and he inspired zeal and enthusiasm that lasted more than one game. In fact he was primarily responsible for a slight change for the better in England's fortunes.

Chapter Seven

The Overseas Challenges 1905–9

On 16 September 1905, the first side sent to the United Kingdom by the New Zealand R.F.U., which had been founded in 1892, beat Devon 55–4 at Exeter. British Rugby has never been quite the same since.

In the understatement of the decade, R.F.U. Secretary Rowland Hill at the end of the tour stated, 'England has been rather slack at Rugby football of late years.' These original All Blacks showed the need for fitness, enthusiasm, dedication and, above all, combination. They believed in the value of quick heeling and breaking. Their forwards, packing 2-3-2, waited for the two 'hookers' and the 'lock' to take up position instead of packing 'first up, first down'.

However, some aspects of their play were unpopular. They were prepared to risk a penalty to save a try and they introduced a new tactic of a 'wing forward' putting the ball in the scrum and obstructing opponents who tried to get round on to the sole New Zealand 'half-back' who waited at the base of the scrum to pass the ball to either of the two five-eighths. There were even complaints that the All Blacks' practice of giving code signals in Maori was unfair play!

By the time these New Zealanders met England they had won all twenty-three matches, including the internationals against Scotland and Ireland, and never in the history of Rugby football had a match in England aroused so much interest. The R.F.U. staged the game at Crystal Palace, then the venue of the F.A. Cup Final. All 15,332 seats in the enclosure were sold a fortnight before and the crowd was estimated at 60,000—a record for a rugger match.

The teams were:

England: E. J. Jackett (Cornwall); A. E. Hind (Midlands), H. Shewring (Somerset), R. E. Godfray (Middlesex), H. Imrie (Durham); J. E. Raphael (Surrey); D. R. Gent (Gloucestershire), J. Braithwaite (Midlands); V. H. Cartwright (Midlands, capt.), C. E. L. Hammond (Middlesex), B. A. Hill (Kent), J. L. Mathias (Gloucestershire), E. W. Roberts (Devon), R. F. Russell (Midlands), G. Summerscales (Durham).

New Zealand: G. Gillett; D. McGregor, R. G. Deans, W. J. Wallace; J. W. Stead, J. Hunter; F. Roberts; D. Gallaher (capt.); J. O'Sullivan, G. Tyler, S. Casey, F. Newton, F. Glasgow, A. McDonald, C. Seeling.

Gallaher occupied the controversial wing forward position and England's answer was to play Raphael as 'rover' with carte blanche to do as he pleased—a tactic that was afterwards agreed to be a mistake.

Although handling the ball was difficult in greasy conditions, the All Blacks scored five tries, four of them by McGregor. They won 15–0 and eventually lost only one of their thirty-three games—to Wales, who gained a famous 3–0 victory at Cardiff.

Jackett, from Falmouth, made a favourable impression at full-back with his high-class fielding, positional sense and ability to find touch 'to a yard', and he was one of only three men to play in all of England's five internationals in 1905–6. The others were the admirable Cartwright, who this season led his club, Nottingham, to their sole Midland Counties Cup triumph, and 'Curly' Hammond, a Harlequins forward noted for his tackling.

Devon won the county championship in 1906 and the seven changes for the Welsh match included the introduction of three typical Devon forwards—T. S. Kelly, W. A. Mills and G. E. Dobbs—all clever, hefty and hardworking, and R. A. Jago at scrum half. Gent, the other half, also worked the scrum for his club—Gloucester, who with 661 points in 37 matches were enjoying a vintage season—and in a trial agreed to play stand-off to Jago until half-time. However, at the interval it was decided it would be foolish to change over and thus, by accident rather than design, England started playing a scrum half and a stand-off rather than a right half and a left half as they had done up to 1905. A new cap for the Welsh match was A. Hudson, a wing over thirteen stone in weight who went for the line with superb dash. In 1905–6 he scored forty-one tries for Gloucester, and he achieved the remarkable feat of running in ten tries in his eight internationals.

Wales, who included thirteen of the men who had upset New Zealand—among them such immortal backs as Nicholls, Gabe, Morgan, Bush and Owen—won 16–3 and at Leicester Ireland won 16–6, so it was back to the drawing board for the Scottish match in Edinburgh.

Amongst the new caps were three players who were to make an indelible mark on England's rugby—J. G. G. Birkett (centre) and A. D. Stoop (stand-off), both Harlequins, and Bridgwater Albion's R. Dibble, a forward of the highest class who represented Somerset seventy-three times between 1901 and 1921. J. 'Darkie' Peters, a coloured scrum half from Plymouth, started a move that led to a try by Raphael; Simpson got clear on the left to score England's second try, and Mills was up for the third, after the massive Birkett had broken through from near his own line, to give England a 9–3 victory—their first win for two years. M. W. Walter, a London Scottish centre who had been selected to play for England this season but declined the invitation because he preferred to accept the offer of a Scottish cap, thus found himself on the losing side!

Rugby had been imported into France in 1872. The U.S.F.S.A. was formed in 1887, and in 1906 France entered the international arena when they entertained New Zealand, who won 38–8. England was the first of the four Home Unions to give them a fixture, and on the Thursday after the Scottish match the same England team, apart from two who could not travel, took the field in Paris. Hudson scored four tries, Kewney, Stoop, Hogarth, Peters and Mills one each, Cartwright converted four, and England won 35–8. Fifty years later a French survivor recalled that he remembered the New Zealand match as a series of black avalanches and the English match as a series of white avalanches!

The following season, 1906–7, saw the arrival of the first Springboks, anxious both to be worthy of following in the All Blacks' footsteps and to promote a better understanding between Briton and Boer, who only a few years previously had been locked in the grim fields of warfare. The only novelty in their play was a 3-3-2 scrum and they often played right and left halves. However they had exceptional weight and pace forward and played brilliantly to their wings. They came to Crystal Palace for the international against England with victories over Wales and Ireland behind them and only one defeat—to Scotland in the mud.

The teams were:

England: E. J. Jackett (Cornwall); F. G. Brooks (East Midlands), J. G. G. Birkett (Surrey), H. E. Shewring (Somerset), T. Simpson (Northumberland); A. D. Stoop (Surrey), R. Jago (Devon); V. H. Cartwright (Midlands, capt.), A. Alcock (Surrey), R. Dibble (Somerset), J. Green (Yorkshire), B. A. Hill (Kent), T. S. Kelly (Devon), W. Mills (Devon), C. H. Shaw (Midlands).

South Africa: S. Joubert; A. W. F. Marsburg, H. de Villiers, S. de Melker, J. Loubser; F. Dobbin, D. Jackson; P. Roos (capt.), D. Brink, W. S. Morkel, D. F. T. Morkel, P. le Roux, H. Daneel, J. Raaff, W. Millar.

England were fortunate to catch the South Africans on treacherous going. All the Springboks had to show for their first-half pressure was a try in the corner by Millar. After the interval Shewring, a Bristol centre, made a 'run worthy of the giants of the past' to secure position near the South African line and Stoop worked the blind side. The ball went loose for Brooks, an Old Bedfordian on leave from Rhodesia (whom he had represented in the 1906 Currie Cup) and playing in his only international, to dive on for a try which brought England a 3–3 draw—their best result against South Africa until 1969.

Then followed the first visit by France. Neither England, who won 41–13, nor the 6,000 crowd at Richmond took the game seriously.

D. Lambert, a Harlequin winger with 'a stride a foot longer than his opponents' ', scored five tries and this remains, alongside G. Lindsay's five for Scotland *v.* Wales in 1887, the most obtained by a man in an international. But Lambert, who was making his debut, was only in the team because the selected wings had cried off injured, and did not keep his place for the next match! Other tries were scored by L. A. N. Slocock, a big fast forward from Liverpool and Lancashire, W. M. Nanson (Carlisle and Cumberland), Shewring and Birkett, who also dropped a goal. B. A. Hill, a Blackheath and Kent forward who had become the first serviceman to captain England, made five conversions.

Despite the exceptional opportunity to build up a team England were outplayed at Swansea and lost 0–22. For the first time England's forwards were given fixed places in the scrum, but this was held to be a handicap rather than a help and for the Irish (lost 9–17) and Scottish (lost 3–8) matches it was back to 'first up, first down'. Scotland had beaten South Africa, Wales and Ireland without having their line crossed and Peters's last-minute try for England was acclaimed as a minor triumph.

After France had been beaten 19–0 at Colombes on New Year's Day 1908, Wales were played on Bristol City F.C.'s ground, Ashton Gate. The 25,000 crowd found the course of play a matter of surmise as a thick fog shrouded the ground. The result was given as England 18, Wales 28.

There was a welcome 13–3 win over Ireland at Richmond in a match marked by the only appearance for England of H. H. Vassall, nephew of the great 'Jumbo'. 'H. H.', who was accident prone, and joined the colonial service on leaving Oxford, had a long raking stride and beautiful swerve which earned him a reputation as a complete centre for the Anglo-Welsh team that played three Tests in New Zealand in 1908, drawing one and losing two.

However, Vassall made one of his numerous cry-offs for the Calcutta Cup match at Edinburgh, and was replaced by W. N. Lapage, a versatile three-quarter who was one of the first products of the Royal Navy R.U., which had been formed in 1907 and which has played the Army every year since. England lost a 10–3 lead and went down 16–10, Scotland's match-winner being K. G. MacLeod, winning his tenth and last cap before retiring at the age of twenty.

The 1908–9 season was marked by the first visit of an Australian touring team, the original Wallabies. They were a great disappointment after the previous colonial sides and accused of employing deliberately unfair means.

The 1908 Olympic games were held in London, and Rugby football was one of the events. Cornwall, who under the captaincy of E. J. Jackett and with the help of other English internationals in B. B. Bennetts, B. Solomon, J. Davey, T. G. Wedge, J. G. Milton and A. J. Wilson had earlier in the year won the county championship for the only time to date, were nominated to represent England in the Olympics. Australia beat them 32–3 in the final and thus became second Olympic rugger champions (for the record, the others were France in 1900 and U.S.A. in 1920 and 1924).

However, when they came to meet England at Blackheath the Australians had already become the first major overseas team to lose in England, the following Midland Counties team having beaten them 16–5 at Leicester: C. B. Leigh; E. Mobbs (both Northampton), E. W. Assinder (Old Edwardians), K. B. Wood (Leicester), A. Heard (Burton); M. Barrowcliffe (Stratford), R. Harrison; P. Fussell, H. Burke (all Northampton), J. G. Cooper (Moseley), C. Franklin (Burton), S. Penny, E. Hobbs (both Leicester), C. T. de Water (Cambridge University), H. G. Howitt (Nottingham).

For the international England included ten new caps under the captaincy of G. H. D'O. 'Torpedo' Lyon, a hard tackling full-back whose playing career was ruined by sea service. The teams were:

England: G. H. D'O. Lyon (Surrey); E. R. Mobbs (Midlands), F. N. Tarr (Oxford), E. W. Assinder (Midlands), B. B. Bennetts (Cornwall); R. H. Williamson (Oxford), A. H. Ashcroft (Cambridge); J. G. Cooper (Midlands), R. Dibble (Somerset), A. L. Kewney (Northumberland), S. H. Penny (Midlands), F. P. Knight (Devon), A. D. Warrington-Morris (Kent), P. J. Down (Somerset), W. L. Oldham (Midlands).

Australia: P. Carmichael; W. Dix, J. Hickey, C. W. Prentice, C. Russell; A. J. McCabe, C. H. McKivatt; K. Gavin, N. E. Row, J. T. Barnett, C. A. Hammond, P. A. McCue, M. McArthur, T. J. Richards, S. Middleton.

Penny, who played over 500 games for Leicester (246 of them consecutive) and 68 for Midland Counties, well deserved this his only cap, and Oldham became Coventry's first English international, but the team was not as strong as the Midlands one that had beaten the Wallabies. After three minutes Mobbs handed off Russell and passed inside to Tarr who repassed to Mobbs for the latter to score, but Australia scored three tries and won 9–3.

The following Saturday at Cardiff Wales won 8–0, but at Leicester England beat France 22–0, F. N. Tarr, a robust centre who timed his passes well, scoring two tries himself on the ground of his home club and making breaks for tries by Mobbs and Simpson.

Ireland were beaten 11–5 in Dublin, A. C. Palmer, a London Hospital wing, scoring two tries and a conversion on his international debut, but Scotland won 18–8 at Richmond after being 8–3 down at half-time. Scotland had refused to play the Australians, as they considered that the payment to the tourists of three shillings a day 'to cover drinks and meals and other legitimate petty expenses' amounted to professionalism and felt so strongly over the issue that at one stage they had cancelled the Calcutta Cup match as they felt that the R.F.U. was condoning professionalism!

Only three men represented England in all five internationals in 1908–9. One was Edgar Mobbs, the Northampton left wing with a high knee action who developed the 'Mobbs punt' over the full-back. In 1914 Mobbs raised his own company from Northampton sportsmen and earned immortality by kicking a rugger ball into No Man's Land and following up when attacking on the Western Front. He was killed in action in 1917 and his memory is perpetuated in the annual match between East Midlands and Barbarians. The other two were both forwards—Dibble, in the process of establishing a pre-Great-War record for a forward of nineteen caps, and A. L. Kewney, a fiery Northumbrian, one of several leading players who had been attracted to the Leicester club. Kewney was held in high respect by Welshmen as their nickname for him—'Kicking Ginger'—showed.

There was, therefore, little to suggest that England was on the threshold of another golden era.

Chapter Eight

Twickenham Magic 1910–14

On 15 January 1910, England played for the first time at her new national enclosure—Twickenham, which had been bought for £5,000 in 1907. It was to prove a lucky ground and England did not lose to a European country there until 1926.

The first to suffer from the Twickenham bogy were Wales, who lost 6–11 before 25,000 to the following XV: W. R. Johnston (Bristol); F. E. Chapman (Westoe), B. Solomon (Redruth), J. G. G. Birkett (Harlequins), R. W. Poulton (Oxford); A. D. Stoop (Harlequins, capt.), D. R. Gent (Gloucester); E. L. Chambers (Bedford), W. Johns (Gloucester), H. Berry (Gloucester), L. Haigh (Manchester), H. J. S. Morton (Blackheath), C. H. Pillman (Blackheath), D. F. Smith (Richmond), L. E. Barrington-Ward (Edinburgh University).

There was a sensational start. Wales kicked off. Stoop gathered and, typically, ran with the ball instead of kicking to touch. From a loose scrum the ball went via Gent, Stoop, Solomon and Birkett to Chapman who scored in the right corner and England were 3–0 up in less than a minute. After Chapman had kicked a penalty, Wales scrambled a try, but Solomon, a temperamental centre who was loath to play away from Cornwall and declined to represent England again, sold a dummy and scored a try which Chapman converted. Wales could only reply with a try and sustained their first defeat by England for twelve years. Chapman, an elusive wing who could sidestep either way, thus had the distinction of scoring the first try, penalty and conversion in international Rugby at Twickenham. He represented Durham, who in 1909 had created a record by appearing in their tenth successive county final.

The Irish match also at Twickenham, was a rude awakening and the pointless draw was described as 'bull versus bull'.

As usual, there was a large proportion of reserves for the French match in Paris—six men made their only appearance of the season for England—but two tries by Hudson, one by Berry, and a conversion by Chapman saw England to an 11–3 win.

At Inverleith there was an unexpected victory over Scotland. After Scotland had taken a 5–0 lead, Birkett burst through to score under the posts, Chapman converting. Stoop started a move in his own half with a dummy and Birkett scored again. Pillman put Berry over, J. A. S. Ritson (a Northern forward) backed up a dribble by Pillman to make the score 14–5, and England had won the international championship for the first time for eighteen years.

Much of the success was due to the new captain—Old Rugbeian Adrian Stoop. Stoop had won his first cap in 1905 when at Oxford but was regarded as injury prone and had not represented England since breaking a collarbone in 1907. A born footballer, quick off the mark, he revolutionized England's Rugby by developing the art of passing as distinct from throwing and by keeping the ball in play whenever possible. His genius had full reign with his beloved Harlequins, whose captain he was from 1906 to 1914, and his fifteen caps were the record for an England half-back until 1922. In 1910 when the 'Quins moved from Wandsworth to Twickenham he had six internationals in the club's back division—himself at stand-off, H. J. Sibree at scrum half, his brother F.M.('Tim') and Birkett at centre and Lambert and Poulton on the wings.

Another source of strength at this time was Gloucestershire, who in 1910 won the county championship for the first time by beating Yorkshire 23–0 in the final. Their captain was scrum half Dai Gent who, like Stoop, would attack from his own 25 and whose knowledge of Welsh was invaluable in matches against the Principality! In fact six Gloucestershire men assisted England in 1910—there were also W. R. Johnston (Bristol), a full back with 'a deadly embrace' hailed as England's best since Gamlin; two three-quarters—A. Hudson (Gloucester) and L. W. Hayward (Cheltenham); and two forwards—H. Berry and W. Johns (both Gloucester).

A great part in England's revival was played by C. H. ('Cherry') Pillman, a twenty-year-old forward from Blackheath and Kent. He made sure that he packed at the back of the scrum on 'the field side'; his aim was to make it impossible for the opposing fly-half to break through and he developed the art of covering so that he frequently caught the wing in possession.

In 1910 came the first tour officially conducted by all four Home Unions. It was to South Africa, and the R.F.U., anxious that it should be a success, requested club committees to notify them of players 'agreeable to make the journey'. The only England regular 'agreeable' was Pillman, who turned out to be the star of the tour, top scoring with 65 points and playing in all three Tests—as fly-half in the second which produced an 8–3 win for Britain. Reviewing the tour, one South African wrote, 'Pillman played a game apparently invented by himself. He would appear as a fly-half, suddenly turn up on the wing and next bob up leading a forward swoop. Every now and then, as if to vary the monotony, he would be seen helping the full-back, but it was his spoiling work that proved such a decisive factor.' The South Africans had seen nothing like it before—they did not play New Zealand until 1921—and to this day Pillman is regarded as the father of Springbok back-row forward play.

Pillman and his ilk were helped by a law change in 1911. Up to that time, when a scrum was screwed a lock could dip his knees, pick up the ball with them and give the order 'right' or 'left' for a wheel, and all eight forwards would push. Henceforth it became illegal to pick up the ball in a scrum between the legs. It was no longer so necessary for the back row of a side that had lost the ball to hang on in case of a wheel and most sides developed at least one spoiling wing forward.

After the triumphs of the previous season, 1911 was an anti-climax.

At Swansea Wales won a great game 15–11. A. D. Roberts, a speedy wing from Northern, opened the scoring with a try on his debut. Wales took a 12–3 lead with three tries and a dropped penalty but Kewney gathered a cross-kick by Roberts and scored under the posts, Lambert converting, and J. A. Scholfield, a Cambridge centre in his only international, slipped outside his winger (an early 'loop') to make the score 12–11. However, Wales made the game safe with a late try.

The next week France paid their first visit to Twickenham. They had already beaten Scotland to record their first international victory but were no match for the Englishmen, who 'showed a becoming sense of humour when illegally detained', and there were 'amusing examples of the Entente Cordiale'. England won 37–0, tries being obtained by Pillman (2), Lambert (2), A. D. Stoop and United Services forwards W. E. Mann and N. A. Wodehouse. 'Daniel' Lambert, as well as being a big, fast wing, could place kick from anywhere and landed five conversions and two penalties to make his personal tally in the match 22. This equalled the international record by D. Mare for South Africa *v.* France in 1907, and only F. McCormick with 24 for New Zealand *v.* Wales in 1969, has ever scored more points in an international. Lambert's career total of 46 points from 7 matches remained the England record up to the Great War.

There was a poor display in Dublin where Ireland won by a try to nil, but the season finished with a victory over Scotland at Twickenham under a new captain—A. L. H. Gotley, a clever little Blackheath scrum half.

For the Scottish match, England had recalled R. W. Poulton, an Old Rugbeian, who had previously played on the wing—the position from which he had scored five tries in Oxford's 35–3 win in the 1909 Varsity match. This time he played left centre, and showed the beautiful running that made him the idol of English Rugby up to the Great War. He ran with his head well back and the ball in both hands at arms' length; he had an instinct for seeing a gap and, thanks to a peculiar trick of crossing his feet without stumbling, the ability to swerve either way without losing speed. He was a Rugby genius and one of the best players to don an England jersey.

With his fellow Harlequins Birkett and A. D. Stoop, England had a midfield triangle ready to take risks. Scotland opened the scoring with a try but Wodehouse replied with a try after good work by Stoop and Birkett. R. O. Lagden, an Oxford forward playing in his only international, converted. Stoop, Poulton and Birkett then made a try for P. W. Lawrie, the Leicester wing, and Birkett himself scored under the posts for Lagden to add the extra points. Scotland could only reply with a late goal and England won 13–8.

It is recorded that a Scottish centre had his shorts removed by the English full-back ten yards out and to cover his embarrassment sat down!

The English full back was S. H. Williams of Newport. On the 1910 tour of South Africa he had earned a reputation for hard tackling and immaculate touch finding. He had gone on the tour as a Welsh nomination but had a dual qualification and on his return was snapped up by England.

Six of England's powerful pack played in all four internationals in 1911. They were the incomparable Pillman; the fearless Kewney; N. A. Wodehouse, a line-out expert from the Royal Navy; L. G. Brown, who had represented Queensland in 1908–9 before coming to Oxford; L. Haigh (Manchester and Lancashire); and a 5 ft 5 in. 'pocket Hercules' from Headingley named J. A. King, who was noted for his hard scrummaging.

In 1912 England shared the international championship with Ireland though they beat them 15–0.

Williams had retired after one season of international football, but W. R. Johnston (Bristol) had regained his old form. He had the gift of extricating himself from difficult situations and his anticipation was such that opponents always seemed to be kicking to him. He played in all the remaining internationals up to the First World War, by when he had collected sixteen caps—a total not exceeded by an England full-back until the arrival of Hiller.

Lambert cried off for the first match (*v.* Wales) and his replacement H. Brougham, a go-for-the-line winger, did so well that he kept his place all season. This meant that Harlequins now had five England three-quarters on their books. There was a new scrum-half, J. A. Pym (Blackheath), a real worker who was lost to the Army in India at the end of the season. The pack, described as 'as fast as England has ever possessed and above average in shoving power', included four newcomers in A. H. MacIlwaine (United Services), J. H. Eddison (Headingley), R. C. Stafford (Bedford) and D. Holland (Devon Albion). Stafford, a schoolboy of eighteen at Bedford Modern, died before the following international season on the threshold of a great career.

A glorious try by Brougham after interpassing with the ubiquitous Pillman was converted by Chapman and Pym slipped over from a scrum to give England an 8–0 win over

Wales. Against Ireland, beaten 15–0, came the remarkable feat of all the three-quarters scoring tries—A. D. Roberts (2), Poulton, Birkett and Brougham one each.

However, at Inverleith Scotland scrummaged in a manner rarely excelled in international football and won 8–3. England's cause was not helped by the loss after ten minutes of King with a broken rib.

The French match in Paris was won 18–8 and J. G. G. Birkett marked his last appearance by scoring his tenth try for England. A powerfully built centre with a strong defence and 'a hand-off like a kicking mule', he was not afraid to test the opposition by running at them, and his twenty-one caps, gained over six seasons, remained the England record until 1923.

The 1912–13 season opened with the visit of the second Springboks. By the time they played England they had beaten Scotland, Ireland and Wales but had become the first South African team to lose in England when the following London team beat them 10–8 at Twickenham:

H. Millett (Guys); H. Brougham, R. W. Poulton, F. M. Stoop (all Harlequins), A. L. Stokes (Guys); W. J. A. Davies (R.N.C. Greenwich), H. J. H. Sibree (Harlequins); W. S. D. Craven, C. H. Pillman, R. L. Pillman, F. H. Lacey, F. Le S. Stone, G. R. Hind (all Blackheath), R. S. Kennedy (Guys), H. C. Michell (Bank of England).

The idea had been to pair the 'Quins backs with the Blackheath forwards, but Birkett and A. D. Stoop had both cried off injured and the latter's place was taken by a naval cadet appearing in his first important match—W. J. A. Davies, who played so well that he forced his way into the national team, which was:

W. R. Johnston (Bristol); C. N. Lowe (Cambridge), F. M. Stoop, R. W. Poulton (both Harlequins), V. H. M. Coates (Bath); W. J. A. Davies (R.N.), W. I. Cheesman (O.M.T.); N. A. Wodehouse (R.N., capt.), J. A. King (Headingley), C. H. Pillman (Blackheath), J. E. Greenwood (Cambridge), L. G. Brown (Oxford), A. L. Kewney (Leicester), S. Smart (Gloucester), J. A. S. Ritson (Edinburgh University).

South Africa fielded:

G. Morkel; J. A. Stegmann, R. Luyt, J. Morkel, E. E. McHardy; F. Luyt, J. D. McCulloch; D. F. T. Morkel (capt.), T. van Vuuren, A. S. Knight, J. A. Francis, J. D. Luyt, S. Ledger, E. H. Shum, W. N. Morkel.

Poulton became the first man to score in an international against these tourists when he broke and, with two swerves, made the South African defence look impotent as he crossed for one of the greatest England tries of all time. Soon after, Poulton made a magnificent swerving run from his own half and looked a certain scorer when he was collared in the right corner. The Springboks rallied and Jack Morkel went over after an interception. In the second half Duggie Morkel, a siege-gun kicker, won the game 9–3 for South Africa, and took away England's unbeaten record at Twickenham, with two penalties from half-way near touch.

But this was an outstanding English team and they went on to their first Triple Crown since 1892 and their first ever Grand Slam, only possible since 1910 when France first played all four home unions.

N. A. Wodehouse, described by W. J. A. Davies as the best forward captain he ever played under, led by precept and example; he was always on the ball and a fine exponent of the 'catch, drop and dribble' technique of breaking through a line-out. In all five internationals he had with him in the pack Pillman, King, Brown, Greenwood (a specialist in the modern fashion of getting backs moving from a line out), Smart and Ritson.

Five of the backs played all five too. Johnston and Poulton were already experienced campaigners. Lowe, a nine-stone right wing who could swerve at full speed, not only tackled his own wing out of the game but was always likely to get across and tackle an opponent on the other side of the pitch, and played in all England's games for the next ten years. Coates, a Cambridge Blue in 1907, was a one-season wonder: his devastating hand-off, which left opponents sprawling, reminded old-timers of Wade and was responsible for most of his six tries this season. Davies with his perfect hands, speed off the mark, eye for an opening, swerve and long touch finding was hailed as the discovery of the year, primarily responsible for England's success.

He had a new cap at scrum-half—W. I. Cheesman, the O.M.T.s' captain, full of grit but prone to wild passes and replaced for the last match by Davies's Navy partner F. E. Oakley, who had a long pass and was a good dribbler. (Scrum-halves were still expected to break from the scrum with the ball at their feet, and Stoop had turned Sibree into a scrum-half for Harlequins because he dribbled so beautifully!)

The home campaign in 1913 opened with an outstanding 12–0 win at Cardiff, England's first ever win there and their first in Wales since 1895. After a pointless first half in which Johnston distinguished himself against the wind and rain, Davies threw a long pass to Coates and the Somerset winger handed off his opponent to cross in the corner for England's first points at Arms Park for twenty years. Greenwood converted. Poulton dropped a goal and then dribbled forty yards for the tireless Pillman to kick over the Welsh line and touch down.

At Twickenham France were out-classed 20–0. Coates scored three tries, Pillman two and Poulton one, Greenwood converting one.

There followed a handsome 15–4 win in Dublin. Coates ran strongly for two tries, Ritson backed up a Davies cut through carried on by Poulton, and Pillman scored after a forward dribble. Greenwood kicked a penalty. Ireland's score—a dropped goal by R. A. Lloyd—was the only one against England in the championship. In fact in the five internationals in 1912–13 the England line was only crossed once—by South Africa.

For the all-important Scottish match, Temple Gurdon and his selectors courageously changed a winning team. Right centre had been a problem all season and Lowe on the wing had only one pass in four games, so the unselfish F. N. Tarr (Leicester) was recalled. However, the game was a poor one and the only score was a try by Brown, the Oxford captain, who was noted for being both a fine scrummager and clever in the loose.

England's triumphant course continued in 1914 under a new captain—the brilliant Poulton. Leadership is a facet of Poulton's play that is often forgotten, but W. J. A. Davies described him as the ideal captain. At this time Poulton was playing for Liverpool, who also had the Irish and Scottish captains (R. A. Lloyd and F. H. Turner) in their ranks—a remarkable record. The new pack leader was H. C. 'Dreadnought' Harrison, a Royal Marine who, under the custom of the time, represented the Navy *v.* the Army when attached to a ship and the Army *v.* the Navy when shore based.

The season opened with a thrilling one-point win over Wales at Twickenham. Wales had one of its toughest packs and it is recorded that their leader, Rev. Alban Davies, 'lifted the Welsh forwards to great heights'—presumably a reference to his persuasive powers and not the earliest mention of illegality in the line-out. So for once it was basically a case of England's three-quarters versus the Welsh forwards.

Wales opened with a dropped goal but Pillman put Brown over and Chapman converted to give England an interval lead of 5–4. Wales went ahead 9–5 but eight minutes from no side Pillman went in under the posts and Chapman's kick won the game 10–9.

Because Davies had been playing badly, England had dropped both him and his partner Oakley for the Welsh match in favour of the Leicester halves F. M. Taylor and G. W. Wood, who this season helped the old Midlands Union win the county championship for the first and last time.

However, Davies and Oakley were reinstated for the remaining internationals, which meant that the Leicester pair were dropped after only one international that had resulted in victory over Wales.

Ireland were 7 points up at Twickenham, but tries by A. D. Roberts and Lowe reduced the deficit to one point at half-time. Pillman put England ahead after a 'spiral run' by Poulton, and Davies sold a couple of dummies before swerving away for a try converted by Chapman. Lowe dashed over in the corner and England won 17–12.

In J. H. D. Watson (Blackheath) England had at last found the ideal centre for Lowe, who scored three tries against Scotland at Inverleith. A try by Poulton and two conversions by H. C. Harrison gave England a 16–6 lead, and though a late Scottish rally brought them a goal and a dropped goal to make the score 16–15, there was no real doubt that England would retain the Triple Crown.

On Easter Monday in Paris, they went on to complete the Grand Slam—if that was in contention in 1914, as Scotland cancelled their fixtures with France because of a riot in Paris in 1913. Poulton, at his brilliant peak, scored four tries. Lowe went in for three more—to make his total for England in 1914 eight. Davies and Watson also crossed and Greenwood converted six out of the nine tries to give England a 39–13 victory.

An interesting selection for the Scottish and French matches was A. J. Dingle, a 1911 Oxford Blue who in the 1913–14 season scored thirty-nine tries for his club (Hartlepool Rovers) and sixteen more for his county (Durham). Regrettably he did not add to his total in the internationals. As usual, England were below strength for their visit to Paris and their team *v.* Scotland for what proved to be the last match against a home union for six years was:

W. R. Johnston (Bristol); C. N. Lowe (Cambridge), J. H. D. Watson (Blackheath), R. W. Poulton (Liverpool, capt.), A. J. Dingle (Hartlepool Rovers); W. J. A. Davies, F. E. Oakley (both U.S. Portsmouth); J. E. Greenwood, A. F. Maynard (both Cambridge), S. Smart (Gloucester), J. Brunton (North Durham), G. Ward (Leicester), L. G. Brown (London Hospital), H. C. Harrison (U.S.), C. H. Pillman (Blackheath).

Poulton, Watson, Dingle, Oakley and Maynard were amongst those killed in the war that started in 1914.

Chapter Nine

Davies and Kershaw 1920–3

International rugby was resumed in 1920, and England continued where they had left off in 1914. In the first five post-war seasons they achieved three Grand Slams and a share in one championship.

However, their first match after the holocaust was not auspicious. At Swansea J. Shea scored 16 points and Wales won 19–5. This game was notable for selectors' whims. W. M. Lowry (Birkenhead Park) was selected on the wing and photographed with the team but was withdrawn just before kick-off in favour of H. L. V. Day (Army) whose style of play was thought to be more suited to the heavy conditions. Day, in fact, scored England's try and converted it.

Four pre-war caps played, but W. J. A. Davies was only selected as reserve, though his new partner for United Services, Portsmouth, and the Royal Navy was included in the team. This was C. A. Kershaw, who also gained fame as a fencer in the 1920 Olympics. Very strong and as fast as most wingers, Kershaw added new dimensions to scrum-half play. No one had ever flashed out passes like Kershaw: the ball came from his hands—sometimes even his feet—like a bullet. He was the first scrum-half to break regularly with the ball in his hands, thus keeping opponents from concentrating unduly on the fly-half. Further, he did not think his work was done when he had got in his pass but tried to be in movements up to the end.

Davies, who practised regularly with Kershaw at Portsmouth, and had the hands to take his 'thunderbolts', was reinstated for the next match and only missed one more international—through injury—before he retired in 1923 when nearly thirty-three.

France, where competitive rugby had been restarted in

1915–16, sent their best side yet and led 3–0, but J. E. Greenwood kicked a penalty and converted a try by Davies to give England an 8–3 victory.

Greenwood was England's first post-war captain. He had won Blues at Cambridge in 1910, 1911, 1912 (as captain) and 1913 and had skippered Old Alleynians. He returned to Cambridge after the war and, the 'four-year' rule being waived to help Varsity rugger get going again, resumed the captaincy in 1919, thus having the remarkable record of five Blues spread over ten years. A genuine forward with the (then) rare knack of catching the ball well above his head and a useful place kicker, Greenwood was of great value in rebuilding England's rugby too.

In Dublin Ireland were leading 11–0 in the second half but Greenwood and his forwards got on top and a fine rally saw tries by Wakefield, Mellish, Myers and Lowe, Cumberlege converting one for England to snatch victory 14–11.

Scotland came to Twickenham having beaten Wales and Ireland and expecting to win the Triple Crown, but England finished the season in a blaze of triumph. Davies was supreme. A natural left-footer, he cross-kicked accurately for Lowe to gather and score and then slipped through the Scottish defence and a long pass saw Harris over. Greenwood converted both tries. After the interval Kershaw broke from a scrum forty yards out to score a try that made the score 13–4 and ensured the first triple tie in the championship, England, Wales and Scotland each finishing with three wins.

After their poor start, England ended the 1920 campaign with a fine side. Full back was B. S. Cumberlege, captain of Blackheath who lost only two of their twenty-six matches in 1919–20 when they supplied six men for England, five of them playing in the Welsh match. Cumberlege, a Cambridge scrum-half pre-war, kicked well with either foot and started attacks from full-back; he later became a leading referee and his sixteen internationals are still the most handled by an Englishman. The wings were both Blackheath—the admirable Lowe, with his wonderful turn of speed, beautiful hands, effective side-step, ability to punt ahead or cross-kick and model defence, and S. W. Harris, clever but not as determined as Lowe.

One centre was E. D. G. Hammett of Newport; Somerset born, he helped that county to its sole championship in 1923.

His positional sense and judgment made up for lack of pace. The other was E. Myers, who had joined Headingley on leaving school in 1913 as there was no Bradford R.U. Club then. After the war he became captain of the newly formed Bradford Club. Cool and collected, Myers seldom made a mistake himself, was unselfish to a degree and was an exemplary tackler.

In front of Davies and Kershaw were forwards who were to become household names.

Outstanding was W. W. Wakefield, a Harlequin who was largely instrumental in founding the Royal Air Force Union in 1919. A complete footballer, he had all the attributes—strength, weight and speed—of a great forward. He was a master of the art of dribbling at pace, was up with his backs to share in an attack and took and gave passes well. Basically, his reputation was as a tight forward with a tremendous shove whose line-out play was nearly in the Wodehouse class, yet he was as fast as many a winger and if a back were injured it was Wakefield who would probably be pulled out of the scrum. His thirty-one caps remained the England record for forty-two years.

Gloucestershire had a hat-trick of county championships in 1920, 1921 and 1922 and three of their forwards represented England in 1920—S. Smart, S. G. Holford and A. T. Voyce. Voyce, one of the first of many 'internationals' from the English Schools Union (founded 1904) to win a senior cap, played the spoiling game to perfection, usually looking after the scrum-half on the blind side. He excelled in the loose, but it was said of him that he never pushed in the scrum except in front of the stand containing the selectors!

Voyce had started on a career that earned him twenty-seven successive caps. Another cornerstone of the England pack to make his debut in 1920 was G. S. Conway, a Cambridge forward who played eighteen times for England. John Daniell described Conway as 'the only British forward between the wars whose footwork would have passed muster with the old-timers'.

F. W. Mellish, an untiring forward from Blackheath, played in all four internationals; he returned to South Africa and proved his class by playing for the Springboks in two Tests in New Zealand in 1921 and in all four against the 1924 British Lions.

There were two debutants in the Scottish match—A. F. Blakiston, a fiery breakaway forward from Northampton, who went on to win seventeen caps, and Stoker T. Woods, a heavyweight forward, and one of the first from the Lower Deck to play in the Inter-Services Tournament, which was only opened to Other Ranks after the war. Woods played for Devonport Services which had been founded in 1919 and took over the old Devon Albion ground, the Albion being forced to combine with Plymouth as Plymouth Albion.

It may be said that 1921 was England's best ever year: they not only won all four matches but scored 61 points and conceded only 9 in the process.

The Welsh match at Twickenham was one-sided, as England were 12 points up after a quarter of an hour. A. M. Smallwood, a wing from Leicester, difficult to stop when under way, ran strongly down the left and passed inside to the faithful Kershaw whose try was converted by Hammett. Davies celebrated his appointment to the England captaincy with a dropped goal and Lowe scored a try. Two tries by Smallwood, one after a clever punt by Hammett, the other after a feint by the same player, gave England an 18–3 win, their biggest over Wales this century.

Before the match England, who had selected four forwards who liked winging, were given no chance against the Welsh heavyweights but the fast forward game paid off and before long was copied by the other countries.

The side, hailed as one of England's greatest, was:

B. S. Cumberlege; C. N. Lowe (both Blackheath), E. D. G. Hammett (Newport), E. Myers (Bradford), A. M. Smallwood (Leicester); W. J. A. Davies (capt.), C. A. Kershaw (both U.S. Portsmouth); R. Edwards (Newport), E. R. Gardner (Devonport Services), L. G. Brown, F. W. Mellish (both Blackheath), T. Woods (Devonport Services), A. F. Blakiston (Northampton), W. W. Wakefield (Harlequins and R.A.F.), A. T. Voyce (Gloucester). It was retained en bloc for the Irish match and only changed for the last two games because of the non-availability of Mellish and Myers and an injury to Gardner.

Ireland at Twickenham were beaten 15–0 in heavy going despite the loss after five minutes of Davies, Myers moving to fly-half and Wakefield into the threes. A Blakiston try gave

England a 3–0 interval lead. Lowe scored after a burst by Mellish. Hammett broke from half-way and found the ubiquitous veteran Brown, recalled to lead the pack after seven years' absence, up for the try. Cumberlege converted and Lowe surprised everyone by dropping a goal.

Scotland, in a match that marked the Golden Jubilee of international rugby, went down 18–0 in a hurricane. Edwards, from Newport (who this season fielded a full XV of internationals), Woods, Brown and Q. E. M. A. King, an Army wing playing in his only international, scored tries, Hammett, a Welsh amateur soccer cap in 1912, converting three.

France in Paris provided a fierce game, but tries by Lowe and Blakiston, both converted by Hammett, ensured a 10–6 win for England, and their third Grand Slam.

The 1922 season was England's least successful campaign in the immediate post-war years. It opened at Cardiff, where Wales won 28–6. Arms Park was a sea of liquid mud but, though the English pack slithered about all over the place, the Welsh forwards kept their feet and revived the dying art of foot passing to each other, soccer style. It transpired that on the morning of the match the Welsh had had new, extra-long studs put in their boots. Fortunately for them the referee did not inspect the boots before the game.

England had been without their lucky mascot W. J. A. Davies, off injured, at Cardiff but for the Irish match in Dublin he returned and England made seven other changes. Kershaw made four breaks and three of them resulted in tries—by Smallwood, Lowe and Gardner. J. E. Maxwell-Hyslop, a new forward from Oxford (who this season won the first Varsity match played at Twickenham, whither the fixture had been transferred after thirty-three years at Queen's Club), also crossed and England won 12–3. This was the match in which an exasperated Irish supporter shouted, 'If you can't catch Davies for heaven's sake ruffle his hair!'

England deserved to lose to France for the first time, but were saved by the magnificent place kicking of H. L. V. Day, who between 1921 and 1928 scored over 1,000 points for Leicester and on this occasion kicked two penalties and converted Voyce's try to snatch an 11–11 draw. The feat was all the more remarkable because, on arriving at Twickenham, Day found he had left his boots in the hotel and borrowed a pair from a reserve, I. J. Pitman (Oxford). Against Scotland Pitman became the first Old Etonian to play for England; two tries by Lowe and one by Davies gave England an 11–5 victory.

A great forward who gained a regular place this season was the Cambridge captain, R. Cove-Smith, an Old Merchant Taylor. Good in the line-out and never happier than when fighting with the ball against three or four opponents, Cove-Smith was a scientific scrummager who could play well anywhere in the pack. He was on a winning England XV a record twenty-two times, and is the only Englishman this century to have captained a Lions tour to South Africa.

Twenty-six men had represented England in 1922, but a settled side emerged again for 1923. The team against Wales at Twickenham was:

F. Gilbert (Devonport Services); C. N. Lowe (Blackheath), E. Myers (Bradford), L. J. Corbett (Bristol), A. M. Smallwood (Leicester); W. J. A. Davies, C. A. Kershaw (both U.S., Portsmouth); W. G. E. Luddington (Devonport Services), R. Edwards (Newport), E. R. Gardner (Devonport Services) *front row*; W. W. Wakefield (Cambridge University), R. Cove-Smith (O.M.T.) *second row*; A. T. Voyce (Gloucester), G. S. Conway (Rugby), H. L. Price (Leicester) *back row.*

Wakefield, in his first full year as pack leader, believed in fixed positions in the scrummage, and 1922–3 was a remarkable season for him. As well as leading the pack when England won all four games, he captained the R.A.F. to its first victory in the inter-services championship and, being on a course at Cambridge, skippered them to a 21–8 win over Oxford!

Wakefield started the international campaign by kicking off against Wales. The ball was blown back into the hands of Price, who dropped for goal and missed. It ran over the Welsh line and Price won the race for the touch down, to give England a 3–0 lead without a Welshman having touched the ball! Wales soon equalized, but twenty minutes after the interval Corbett, finding himself hemmed in, passed the ball between his legs to Smallwood, who dropped an amazing goal from near touch a few yards inside the Welsh half to win the match for England 7–3.

The same side was selected en bloc for Ireland at Leicester, but Edwards cried off and was replaced by F. W. Sanders, the

Plymouth Albion hooker. This, the last home international not staged at Twickenham, resulted in an easy 23–5 win for England. Davies dropped a goal. Smallwood rounded off a move with a try. Corbett sold a dummy and scored. Price crossed from a line-out, Conway converting. Lowe appeared on the left wing and sprinted over for Conway to convert, and Voyce, typically, appeared from nowhere to score after the ball had gone out to the wing and back in-field.

For the visit to Scotland, who had already won all three games, T. E. Holliday (Aspatria and Cumberland) replaced the injured Gilbert who had won two caps at the age of thirty-nine. Corbett was dropped for over-indulgence in the dummy in favour of H. M. Locke, the Birkenhead Park centre, and A. F. Blakiston (Northampton) was recalled to the exclusion of Price. Though Price had scored in both the internationals, his Pillman type of roving was not appreciated by everyone.

Smallwood put England ahead by showing an unsuspected turn of speed, but Scotland scored two tries to lead 6–3. Locke intercepted and Voyce gathered his kick ahead to score in the corner.

England's place kicking against Wales and Ireland had been disastrous, and Luddington had been instructed to practise the fortnight before the match. The Devonport Services secretary reported that Luddington had practised daily and added that it was important for his club-mate, Gardner, to place the ball, not Kershaw. Gardner placed the ball carefully and Luddington's long kick went over to give England the Triple Crown by 8 points to 6.

The same side beat France 12–3 at Colombes on Easter Monday. After a French penalty, Wakefield picked up and went over. Conway sprinted forty yards for a try and with almost the last kick of the game Davies dropped a goal to ensure another Grand Slam.

Davies was carried off the field shoulder high, for this was his last international. He retired with the incredible record of having played twenty-two times for England and helped them to twenty wins and one draw. The only time he was on the losing side was his first international—against the 1912 Springboks—and he had played for London when they beat *them.*

In a tribute to him, James Baxter, the Chairman of the English Selection Committee, wrote:

> Not only is W. J. A. Davies the greatest match-winner who ever put on a football boot, but as captain of the national XV he was essentially the right man in the right place. Idolized by the men under him . . . his lovable personality and intense enthusiasm for the game marked him out as the ideal captain. No player was ever more closely marked . . . but nothing ever ruffled him. All he did was done at express speed—his drop at goal, his cut through, his kick to touch, his passing, all happened so quickly that the opposing forces were often left standing in sheer bewilderment. Internationals of more than one country have for years expressed their opinion that they would never beat England as long as Davies played, and they spoke the truth.

Cyril Lowe, the right-winger par excellence, also decided to call it a day. His twenty-five caps had set a new record for England; his appearances had been consecutive and war had deprived him of five years' international rugby—and another twenty caps! His eighteen tries for his country are still England's record.

Kershaw, too, never played for England again as he was posted to sea. He and Davies had played together for England fourteen times. Their record of thirteen wins, one draw and no losses makes them the most successful pair of halves the world of international rugby has ever seen—or is ever likely to see.

Chapter Ten

More Grand Slams 1924–8

Because of the loss of Davies, Kershaw and Lowe, England were not expected to do well in 1924. But it is forwards who win matches. The pack had laid the foundation of England's successes in 1921 and 1923 and England could still command the services of some of the finest forwards they have ever had in Wakefield, Cove-Smith, Voyce, Conway, Blakiston, Luddington and Edwards.

Except that C. K. T. Faithful (Harlequins) replaced an injured Edwards for the Irish match, these seven played together in all the 1924 internationals with A. Robson (Northern) hooking.

The new halves were Myers, moved from centre, and the brilliant, if erratic, Cambridge scrum-half A. T. Young. Only 5 ft 5 in., and known as 'the little man', Young was as slippery as an eel and had the courage of a tiger. He had a fine positional sense and one international opponent said, 'Whenever we kicked a blade of grass, there was Arthur Young behind it.'

Corbett and Locke established themselves as a fully equipped pair of centres, and there were new wings in H. C. Catcheside (Percy Park) and H. P. Jacob (Oxford University). Catcheside's pace brought him two tries in each of his first two internationals and one in each of the other two, to make his total for the season six. Jacob, who had a deceptive swerve, became the only Englishman between the wars to score three tries in a match when he did the 'hat-trick' against France. Jacob's ability was such that the famous 'Oxford-Scottish' three-quarter line of A. C. Wallace, G. Aitken, G. P. S. MacPherson and I. S. Smith, who were largely responsible for Scotland's only Grand Slam (in 1925), never appeared together in the Varsity match because a place always had to be found for Jacob!

Rugby at The Oval—England *v.* Scotland, 1872

Top 1886 Temple Gurdon's last match. E. T. Gurdon's 16 appearances was the England record for 25 years. He captained England in nine matches, eight of which were won and the other drawn. His team included two of the game's pioneers—Alan Rotherham, the first half to link forwards and three-quarters, and R. Robertshaw, the first centre to play to his wings. *Back row* (left to right)*:* A. E. Stoddart, F. Bonsor, A. Teggin, E. B. Brutton. *Second row:* C. Gurdon, Alan Rotherham, W. G. Clibborn, N. Spurling, R. Robertshaw. *Seated:* R. E. Inglis, E. T. Gurdon (captain), E. Wilkinson, C. J. B. Marriott. *In front:* C. H. Sample, G. L. Jeffery.

Left 1892: Before the split. England's last Triple Crown XV for 21 years—and the only side from any country to win a Triple Crown without conceding a point. *Standing* (left to right): H. Varley, W. Yiend, T. Kent, W. E. Bromet, E. Bullogh, W. Nichol, J. Toothill. *Seated:* F. Evershed, S. M. J. Woods, F. H. R. Alderson (captain), J. Dyson, R. E. Lockwood, H. Bradshaw. *In front:* A. Briggs, J. Coop.

Above Rugby at Crystal Palace—England 3, South Africa 3, 1906

R.F.U.
ENGLAND v WALES
15TH JAN 1910

H. BERRY

E.L. CHAMBERS

L. HAIGH

W. JOHNS

D.R. GENT

R.W. POULTON

B. SOLOMON

A.D. STOOP (CAPT.)

F.E. CHAPMAN

J.G.G. BIRKETT

W.R. JOHNSTON

H.J.S. MORTON

C.H. PILLMAN

D.F. SMITH

L.E. BARRINGTON-WARD

ENGLAND
1 GOAL FROM A TRY
1 PENALTY GOAL
1 TRY
11 POINTS

WALES
2 TRIES
6 POINTS

Left The first England XV to play at Twickenham. (Unfortunately no group photograph was taken of this team.)
Top The first Grand Slam team—1913. *Standing* (left to right): W. I. Cheesman, F. E. Steinthal, S. Smart, J. A. S. Ritson, J. E. Greenwood, V. H. M. Coates, G. Ward, W. J. A. Davies. *Seated*: L. G. Brown, C. H. Pillman, R. W. Poulton, N. A. Wodehouse (captain), W. R. Johnston, J. A. King, C. N. Lowe.
Above Davies's men—the 1921 Grand Slam XV prior to beating Wales 18–3 at Twickenham. *Standing* (left to right): E. R. Gardner, T. Woods, E. Myers, A. T. Voyce, A. F. Blakiston, A. M. Smallwood, F. W. Mellish, B. S. Cumberlege. *Seated:* E. D. G. Hammett, R. Edwards, L. G. Brown, W. J. A. Davies (captain), C. N. Lowe, W. W. Wakefield. *In front:* C. A. Kershaw.

Top On the way to the 1923 Grand Slam. England 8, Scotland 6, at Inverleith. English players (left to right): W. W. Wakefield, C. N. Lowe (back to camera), H. M. Locke, R. Cove-Smith, A. T. Voyce, E. Myers, C. A. Kershaw (with ball).
Left W. J. A. Davies, England's greatest player. Davies played for England in 22 internationals of which 20 were won, one drawn and only one lost (to South Africa in 1912). He was a member of four Grand Slam teams. His record of captaining 10 winning England sides still stands.
Above Wakefield's men—the Grand Slam XV of 1924 prior to beating Wales 17–9 at Swansea. *Standing* (left to right): H. C. Catcheside, B. S. Chantrill, H. P. Jacob, R. Cove-Smith, A. F. Blakiston, H. M. Locke, A. W. Angers (referee). *Seated:* G. S. Conway, R. Edwards, A. T. Voyce, W. W. Wakefield (captain), E. Myers, L. J. Corbett, W. G. E. Luddington. *In front:* A. Robson, A. T. Young.

Top Cove-Smith's men—the five wins in a season team of 1927–8. *Standing* (left to right)*:* A. E. Freethy (referee), K. J. Stark, W. J. Taylor, J. V. Richardson, C. D. Aarvold, J. Hanley, F. D. Prentice, G. V. Palmer. *Seated:* R. H. Sparks, E. Stanbury, R. Cove-Smith (captain), J. S. Tucker, H. G. Periton, K. A. Sellar. *In front:* H. C. C. Laird, A. T. Young.
Above 1934 England 6, Scotland 3. The Triple Crown pack win good ball for their captain and scrum half, B. C. Gadney. English forwards (left to right): H. Rew, J. W. Forrest, G. G. Gregory, R. J. Longland, H. A. Fry, W. H. Weston, D. A. Kendrew, J. Dicks. No 11 is G. W. C. Meikle who scored 4 tries in England's 3 games this season.

R. H. Hamilton-Wickes, a Harlequin winger, came in for the Irish match instead of Locke (injured) and his inclusion meant that all the Cambridge captains from 1920 to 1924 (Conway, Cove-Smith, Wakefield, Hamilton-Wickes and Young) were in the same England team.

Full back for all matches was B. S. Chantrill (Bristol) and England called on only seventeen men throughout the campaign.

The season began with the first win in Wales since 1913—and the first at Swansea for twenty-nine years. Conditions were heavy but the English pack, inspired by the new captain, Wakefield, held their own, and Wales were outclassed behind. Wales scored first but tries by Myers, Jacob and Locke, one converted by Conway, gave England an 11–3 lead at half-time. Catcheside put them further ahead and, after two Welsh tries had closed the gap, made the most of an opening by Corbett to make the final score 17–9.

In the first international at Ravenhill, Belfast, Ireland were beaten 14–3. Ireland equalized an early try by Corbett but after the interval England ran away with the game with one try by Hamilton-Wickes and two by Catcheside, the second after a run from his own line.

England's backs played delightful football against France at Twickenham. Jacob got his hat-trick of tries; Catcheside, finding himself hemmed in, jumped high over the French full back to score; Young dashed over after a typical blind side break and England won 19–7.

The season ended with a 19–0 victory over Scotland at Twickenham. Wakefield won the touch down after a cross-kick by Corbett and Conway converted. After the interval Chantrill thrice brought down I. S. Smith when the 'Flying Scotsman'—his twenty-three tries for Scotland remain the record for international rugby—looked certain to score and England added to their lead with a dropped goal and a try by Myers and a try by Catcheside, using a useful hand-off. Thus England completed their fifth Grand Slam and, remarkably, sixteen of their seventeen tries were scored by backs. It was unfortunate that only four of this triumphant English XV—R. Cove-Smith (as captain), A. F. Blakiston, A. T. Voyce and A. T. Young—could accept invitations to tour South Africa with the 1924 British Lions who, with a more representative party, must surely have returned with a better record than one draw in four Tests.

In January 1925, New Zealand met England in what was regarded as the match of the decade. The gates at Twickenham were closed with 60,000 inside the ground. These Second All Blacks had won all their twenty-seven games, including Wales 19–0 and Ireland 6–0 (they did not play Scotland), and it had long been obvious that if anyone was to halt their progress it would be England, the European champions.

England had all their 1924 Grand Slam team available but the selectors panicked and promoted seven of the Rest side who beat England in the trial. Thus England fielded the following scratch side against the only tourists to win all their matches (thirty) in Britain and France:

J. Brough (Silloth); R. H. Hamilton-Wickes, V. G. Davies (both Harlequins), L. J. Corbett (Bristol), J. C. Gibbs (Harlequins); H. J. Kittermaster (Oxford), A. T. Young (Cambridge); R. Edwards (Newport), J. S. Tucker (Bristol), R. J. Hillard (Oxford), W. W. Wakefield (Harlequins), R. Cove-Smith (O.M.T.), A. F. Blakiston (Liverpool), G. S. Conway (Rugby), A. T. Voyce (Gloucester).

New Zealand: G. Nepia; J. Steel, A. E. Cooke, K. S. Svenson; N. P. McGregor, M. F. Nicholls; J. J. Mill, J. H. Parker; Q. Donald, W. R. Irvine, M. J. Brownlie, R. R. Masters, C. J. Brownlie, A. White, J. Richardson.

After ten minutes the All Blacks lost C. J. Brownlie, sent off for deliberately kicking an opponent, and England took the lead when, following a wheel and forward rush, Voyce foot-passed to Cove-Smith who fell on the ball for a try. But by half-time New Zealand had obtained tries by Svenson and Steel and a penalty by Nicholls. Tries by M. Brownlie and Parker, one converted, gave the All Blacks a 17–3 lead. In the closing stages Corbett dropped a penalty goal and Kittermaster scored a memorable try after backing up a break from his own line by Hamilton-Wickes. Conway converted to make the final score 17–11.

Hamilton-Wickes was one of the few successes in what turned out to be a disappointing season for England. A tall, well built right wing three-quarter with plenty of determination and a wonderful swerve, he had a big part in the 12–6 win over Wales, starting two movements that led to tries and finishing off another.

Amongst the five changes made by England for the Welsh game were the inclusion of H. G. Periton, a tireless loose forward and the first England cap from the Waterloo club, which was becoming a force in Lancashire, and E. J. Massey, a scrum half from Leicester who, as Leicestershire, won the county championship in 1925, the first member of the Midland group (created in 1920) to do so.

Another Leicester and Leicestershire man, A. M. Smallwood, was recalled to the wing for the Irish and Scottish matches. He had had the remarkable record of being on the winning side in each of his ten previous appearances for England, but Ireland, drawing 6–6, came within an ace of being the first European country to win at Twickenham and, in the first international at Murrayfield, Scotland's 14–11 victory meant that they regained the Calcutta Cup for the first time since 1912.

For their 13–11 win in Paris on Easter Monday, England had to thank Luddington who, when a French back missed touch, marked the ball and kicked a goal.

This put England joint second in the 1925 International Championship but in 1926 they sank to fourth. The season opened with a 3–3 draw at Cardiff. Wakefield, breaking Lowe's record by making his twenty-sixth appearance for England, celebrated by scoring England's try.

Ireland had not beaten England since 1911 but in 1926 had in their team some of their most famous players, including G. V. Stephenson (whose 42 caps were the British record until it was broken by K. Jones of Wales in 1956), E. O'D. Davy (34 caps), W. E. Crawford (30), J. D. Clinch (30), J. L. Farrell (29) and M. Sugden (28), and at Lansdowne Road won a thrilling game 19–15.

France were duly beaten 11–0, but Scotland broke the 'Twickenham spell' by becoming the first home country to win there since the ground was opened sixteen years before. The score was 17–9 and contemporary criticism was caustic. C. A. Kershaw wrote, 'Two things, lack of confidence and in a lesser degree lack of physical fitness, cost England very dear.' Only eight players appeared in all four internationals in 1926.

Wakefield and Voyce, in his last international season, of the old brigade kept their places throughout as did J. S. Tucker, first in a long line of specialist Bristol hookers which extends to Pullin, and R. J. Hanvey (Aspatria) who in 1924 had helped Cumberland to its first, and last, county championship. The continued inability to find a first-class full-back was rather disconcerting and the only backs to last the season were Kittermaster at fly-half and two new centres—A. R. Aslett, a splendid tackler from Richmond and the Army, and T. E. S. Francis. Francis was a member of the 1925 Cambridge XV whose 33–3 victory remains Oxford's heaviest defeat in the Varsity match. W. E. Tucker, the Cambridge skipper and a forward like his father (also 'W. E.' and capped thirty-one years previously), and Sir T. G. Devitt, a wing, also played for England this season, and C. D. Aarvold, C. C. Bishop and W. H. Sobey from the Cambridge XV were subsequently capped.

England flattered to deceive in 1927. Wales were beaten 11–9 at Twickenham. Corbett, the new captain, had such an outstanding game that one report claimed, 'It is doubtful if England have ever had a better skipper.' He started by dropping a magnificent goal from a mark. Wales replied with two tries but E. Stanbury, a robust front-row forward from Plymouth Albion who could place kick, landed a penalty and converted a try scored by Corbett after a change of direction and half-dummy. In the second half the only score was a Welsh penalty. Penalty goals appear much more frequently from this time onwards as a change of law in 1925 had allowed the kicker to place the ball himself and banned charging by the offending side who, however, did not have to retire ten yards until 1937.

Ireland at Twickenham took the lead with a penalty, but P. H. Davies, a forward gaining a first English cap for Sale, pounced on an Irish error and put H. C. C. Laird, a strong, bustling, 18-year-old Harlequins stand-off half, over for Stanbury to convert. Ireland regained the lead with a try, but Young sent J. C. Gibbs, a flying Harlequins left-winger, in for the winning try (8–6). This was described as 'Young's match'; despite a head injury, he borrowed Stanbury's scrum cap and was here, there and everywhere, tricking his way through half the Irish team or saving rushes. This year Gibbs,

Young and two newly capped forwards—W. C. T. Eyres (R.N.C. Greenwich) and W. E. Pratten (Blackheath)—helped Kent become the first south-eastern county to win the championship since they had won it themselves in 1904.

At Murrayfield 80,000 saw Scotland win deservedly 21–13, and the season ended lamentably in Paris with France winning by a try to nil and so registering their first victory over England at their seventeenth attempt. This proved to be Wakefield's last international, his thirty-first, though he was far from finished as a player. In 1926 the Middlesex Seven-a-side Tournament was started at Twickenham: Harlequins won the first four competitions, each winning seven including Wakefield, and in 1929 he led Middlesex to their first county championship.

The omens, then, were not good for 1927–8, but England for the only time to date won *five* internationals in a season—the Grand Slam plus a touring side. The only other country to have performed this feat is Wales, who in 1908–9 and again in 1975–6 defeated the four European countries and Australia.

Rugby Union almost died in Australia in the 1920s, and internationals were undertaken by New South Wales. In 1927–8 they had a full tour of Britain and France and came to Twickenham boasting wins over Wales and Ireland.

The teams were:

England: K. A. Sellar (U.S.); W. J. Taylor (Blackheath), C. D. Aarvold (Cambridge), J. V. Richardson (Birkenhead Park), Sir T. G. Devitt (Blackheath); H. C. C. Laird (Harlequins), A. T. Young (Blackheath); E. Stanbury (Plymouth Albion), J. S. Tucker (Bristol), R. Cove-Smith (O.M.T.), D. Turquand-Young (Richmond), K. J. Stark (Old Alleynians), T. M. Lawson (Workington), T. Coulson (Coventry), H. G. Periton (Waterloo).

New South Wales: A. W. Ross; E. E. Ford, C. H. T. Towers, S. C. King, A. C. Wallace; A. T. Lawton, S. J. Malcolm; J. W. Breckenridge, A. N. Finlay, J. G. Blackwood, J. A. Ford, G. P. Storey, B. Judd, E. N. Greatorex, H. F. Woods.

England, who had five new caps and were skippered for the first time by Cove-Smith (four years after he had captained the Lions in South Africa), opened with a try by Tucker after a cross kick by Laird. Richardson, an Oxford Blue in 1925, converted. The 'Waratahs', as these tourists were called, replied with a try by Towers converted by Lawton, but Richardson converted tries by Taylor and Laird for England to lead 15–5 at the interval. The England forwards were excellent in the loose and Periton touched down. New South Wales scored twice in the last quarter but England won 18–11—their first victory over a touring team since the 1889 Maoris!

J. Hanley, a fine wing forward from Plymouth Albion, replaced Periton for the Welsh match at Swansea, where, in bad conditions, England gained an early 10–0 lead with tries by Taylor and Laird, both converted by Richardson—and hung on to it. The half-time score was 10–3. Wales could only score a converted try after the interval and lost 8–10. Sellar, the Navy full-back, played the game of his life and his tackling kept the Welsh out so effectively that he was compared with Gamlin.

Devitt was ill for the trip to Dublin and his place on the wing was taken by G. V. Palmer (Richmond). There were two new caps in the pack—R. H. Sparks, a hooker from Plymouth Albion, then regarded as a nursery for forwards, and F. D. Prentice (Leicester). Prentice's three caps for England this season were his only ones, although in 1930 he captained the only Lions team to visit New Zealand between the wars. He was later well known as R.F.U. Secretary.

With the benefit of a gale in the first half Ireland led 3–0 at the interval, and scored a try soon after. Richardson went over for a try and coolly dropped a goal to give England a 7–6 win.

There were no changes for the French match at Twickenham. Palmer, a pacey winger, scored two tries as did Periton, in magnificent form as blind-side wing forward. Richardson converted three and England won 18–8.

Sellar was ill for the Scottish match and T. W. Brown became the fourth Bristol full-back to represent England since the great Johnston in 1914. The English pack was much heavier than the Scottish despite the presence of the redoubtable J. M. Bannerman, whose thirty-seven caps were the Scottish record until 1962, and Cove-Smith opted for scrums instead of lines-out. Laird forced his way over in the corner and Hanley scored after a break by Young.

England had won 6–0, regained the Calcutta Cup, won the

Triple Crown, achieved the Grand Slam and registered their fifth victory of the season.

They owed much to their pack and to the goal kicking of Richardson who scored 23 of their 59 points and disappeared from the international scene having helped England to wins in each of the five matches he played for them.

Chapter Eleven

Ups and Downs 1929–33

In spite of the excellent results in 1928, there followed a period when England's fortunes fluctuated violently, and in 1929 they slumped to fourth.

Sea service meant that Sellar's international career was finished and Brown, his successor as full-back, proved fallible at times. Palmer had retired, Richardson and Taylor had lost their form and only Aarvold, the Cambridge centre and captain, remained of the three-quarters. His Varsity colleague R. W. Smeddle, also formerly Durham School, was given the right-wing berth on the strength of having scored three tries against Oxford. The left wing pair were G. S. Wilson (Manchester), who had come to the fore helping Lancashire (captained by Periton) win the northern group for the first time since 1891, and G. M. Sladen (Royal Navy), but A. R. Aslett and A. L. Novis, two Army three-quarters, appeared in the last two matches.

There were a different pair of halves for each match and only Stanbury and Periton of the forwards played in all four games, with Turquand-Young playing in the last three. 'Turkey', 6 ft 1 in. in height, was one of the new type of second-row men needed since a law change in 1925 had required the ball to be thrown at least five yards at lines out and thus stopped the old bunching on the touchline. A side effect of the change was that wingers, not scrum-halves, began throwing the ball in.

H. Wilkinson (Halifax), son of the man who played against the 1888 Maoris, gained belated recognition for helping Yorkshire in 1926 and 1928 to its first championships since 1896. A fast, attacking wing forward, noted for being up for the final pass, he marked his debut by scoring both tries against Wales at Twickenham, the first after the speed and swerve of Aarvold had defied tacklers and the second after Laird, soon to go down with tuberculosis, broke from half-way. Wilson converted one to give England an 8–3 victory.

Wilson's conversion of a try by Smeddle gave England a 5–3 lead over Ireland, but Sugden dummied his way over for Ireland to win at Twickenham for the first time, and the England selectors reacted by making seven changes and ending the international careers of Cove-Smith and Young.

Novis and S. S. C. Meikle, a Waterloo fly-half gaining his only cap, both scored tries on debut, but Scotland won 12–6 and the new caps for the match in Paris included two backs who had just assisted Middlesex to its first championship—J. S. R. Reeve (Harlequins) on the wing and R. S. Spong (Old Milhillians) at stand-off.

England won 16–6, thus avoiding a share in the wooden spoon, and it was a surprise when a very experimental side won the international championship in 1930.

There were no fewer than nine new caps in the team that tackled Wales at Cardiff. H. Rew (Exeter and the Army) was due to hook but was taken ill the morning of the match. John Daniell, the England selector, rang Bristol where Sam Tucker was working and ordered him to hire an aeroplane—an unprecedented action in 1930. The plane circled Arms Park to announce its arrival, then landed near by, and Tucker was rushed to the ground just in time for the kick-off. He hooked so well that he not only kept his place for all the matches but finished the season as England's captain! N. W. Matthews (Bath), the travelling reserve, was photographed with the team but never capped.

Reeve scored two tries in the 11–3 win over Wales. A try by Novis had given England a 3–0 half-time lead in Dublin but Ireland won the game 4–3 with a dropped goal. France were beaten 11–5, M. Robson, a centre whose try and dropped goal had won the 1929 Varsity match for Oxford, scoring the best individual try seen at Twickenham for years.

The Calcutta Cup game was a pointless draw, but England's five points from four games sufficed to give them the championship as three weeks later Wales kindly beat France, who needed a win to become champions for the first time.

The regulars who won England this unexpected championship had as full-back J. G. Askew, whom Cambridge had converted from a centre with excellent results. Aarvold was not available and F. W. S. Malir, one of two Otley men capped this season, played centre alongside the opportunist Robson in three matches with Reeve and Novis on the wings.

The first-choice halves were the Old Milhillians R. S. Spong, a strong stand-off, and W. H. Sobey, a scrum-half with a long, accurate pass and a sudden burst. In the front row with Tucker were A. H. Bateson (Otley) and D. A. Kendrew from the new Woodford club (only formed in 1924) or H. Rew. J. W. Forrest (United Services) and B. H. Black, an Oxford South African, were described as England's best second row for years, and Black was also an outstanding long-distance place kicker. Periton and P. D. Howard (Oxford) played in the back row in all matches.

As European champions, England provided sixteen of the British Isles team to tour New Zealand in 1930. Black, with 63, was leading points-scorer in New Zealand and Novis, with 13, scored most tries. Aarvold was acting captain of the side that won the first Test 6–3 at Dunedin—the first British Test victory in New Zealand (and the last till 1959). New Zealand never really recovered from the shock of being 3–0 down after seven minutes, Reeve scoring in the corner after a cross kick by Spong.

Unfortunately, the brilliant Sobey was badly injured in his first match in New Zealand and England had to find a new pair of halves for 1931, when they hit rock-bottom by occupying fifth position in the championship for the first time.

Only a draw with the ultimate champions, Wales, who could still not beat the Twickenham bogy, prevented the ignominy of being whitewashed.

The match had its share of memorable incidents. Powell, the Welsh scrum half, made a mark, placed the ball himself, walked back and took his time. Instead of charging, the mesmerized English watched him kick a goal! England had two new centres in D. W. Burland (Bristol) and M. A. McCanlis (Gloucester), who played together for the Gloucestershire sides that won the county championship in 1930, 1931 and 1932. Burland caught the ball from a long Welsh throw-in and scored a try to make the score 6–6. The touch judges disagreed over Burland's conversion but the referee awarded it. As, at this time, play after both converted and unconverted tries started with a place kick from half-way, many in the crowd, including the scoreboard operator, thought the conversion had been disallowed and at half-time the referee had the scoreboard altered to show England leading 8–6. A direct result of this affair was that since 1934 play after an unconverted try has been restarted by a drop-out from half-way. Five minutes from the end Morley wriggled over for Wales and Bassett converted. Many spectators had left the ground thinking Wales had won 11–8 when, in injury time, Wales were caught offside two yards in their own half, half-way between the centre and right touch, and Black landed his second long-range penalty of the match to snatch an 11–11 draw!

The England selectors regarded the result as lucky and brought in six new caps for the Irish match, among them A. C. Harrison, an auburn-haired little wing from Hartlepool Rovers who 'nosed about like a terrier for an opening', P. C. Hordern, an intelligent forward who had won an Oxford Blue in 1928 and was playing for Newport, and P. E. Dunkley (Harlequins), in 1931 a member of the first Warwickshire pack to reach the county final. After twenty-seven games for England —a total that put him into joint third place after Wakefield and Cove-Smith—Tucker lost his place as hooker to G. G. Gregory (Taunton) and the captaincy to Howard who was in brilliant form in the middle of the back row or 'lock' as the position was then called.

Ireland won 6–5, their third successive victory over England by one point, and there were six changes for the visit to Murrayfield where Scotland won 28–19. J. A. Tallent, a Cambridge centre with an eye for an opening, scored two tries on his debut, and Reeve also crossed twice, the second time after clever work by E. B. Pope, a Blackheath scrum half in the Young mould.

However, Reeve was amongst those axed for the last match—France in Paris—and no fewer than 17 new caps were awarded by England this season. 'Owing to the unsatisfactory state of Rugby football in France,' the four Home Unions had already decided to break off relations with France, 'until we are satisfied that the control and conduct of the game has been placed on a satisfactory basis in all essentials.' France, therefore, had everything to play for and duly won 14–13, despite some more good place kicking by Black who ended the 1931 season with 22 points for England.

Thus between 1932 and 1946 the 'Grand Slam' was not in contention and, unless there was a touring team, the home countries had only three games a season.

However, in 1931–2 there was a touring side—the Third Springboks, the only South African team to visit Britain between the wars. They relied on giant forwards, who packed 3-4-1 and concentrated on an enormous shove, and the 'tactical' kicking of their captain Benny Osler.

On their tour they lost only one of their twenty-six games—at Leicester, to Leicestershire and East Midlands who won one of the most extraordinary games ever seen in England.

The home side was:

R. J. Barr; J. T. Hardwick, R. A. Buckingham (all Leicester), R. C. Brumwell, L. G. Ashwell (both Bedford); C. Slow (Northampton), B. C. Gadney; A. H. Greenwood, D. J. Norman (all Leicester), R. J. Longland, T. Harris (both Northampton), A. S. Roncoroni (West Herts.), E. Coley (Northampton), G. R. Beamish (Leicester, capt.), W. H. Weston (Northampton).

The scoring went: Slow dropped goal. Springboks try. Slow try, Weston converted. Slow try, Weston converted. Springboks try. Hardwick try, Weston converted. Half-time: Midlands 19, South Africans 6. Springboks try. Longland try, Weston converted (24–9). Springboks try, dropped goal and converted try (24–21). Weston penalty. Buckingham try. Result: Midlands 30, South Africans 21.

The Midlands' 30 was, and still is, the most points ever scored against a Springboks team anywhere in the world.

Gadney, Longland and Weston went on to distinguished international careers and, when they assisted England to defeat New Zealand at Twickenham in 1936, became the only men to have played for sides that beat the Third Springboks and the Third All Blacks. However, they were not included in the England XV that met South Africa:

R. J. Barr (Leicester); C. C. Tanner (Gloucester), J. A. Tallent (Cambridge), R. A. Gerrard (Bath), C. D. Aarvold (Blackheath, capt.); R. S. Spong, W. H. Sobey (both Old Milhillians); A. D. Carpenter (Gloucester), D. J. Norman (Leicester), G. G. Gregory (Bristol), C. Webb (Devonport Services), R. G. S. Hobbs (Army and Richmond), L. E. Saxby

(Gloucester), A. J. Rowley (Coventry), J. McD. Hodgson (Northern).

South Africa: G. Brand; M. Zimmerman, B. G. Gray, F. Waring, J. H. van der Westhuizen; B. L. Osler (capt.), P. de Villiers; M. M. Louw, H. G. Kipling, P. J. Mostert, G. M. Daneel, F. Bergh, P. J. Nel, L. C. Strachan, J. A. J. McDonald.

England had picked three hookers as their front row and the South African forwards walked over the ball. England spent much time in their own 25, and, if Osler had not been obsessed with kicking, must have conceded more than one try—and that a debatable one by Bergh after the referee had decided that Barr had not touched down properly. Two minutes from no-side Brand made the score 7–0 with a huge dropped goal.

It was much the same story at Swansea where the English front row buckled and Wales won 12–5.

Spong and Sobey, who had had no chance in either match behind beaten packs, gave way to Sub-Lieut. W. Elliot, one of the many servicemen who helped Hampshire (with U.S. Portsmouth and Aldershot Services in its area) win the South Eastern group this season and its first championship in 1933, and B. C. Gadney, a big scrum half who had been one of the stars of the Midlands win over the Springboks. The only men to play in all four internationals were Aarvold and Tanner on the wings, Gerrard in the centre, the heavyweight second row of Hobbs (son of R.F.A., another Army forward who played for England in 1899 and 1903) and Marine Webb and wing forward Hodgson, newly capped by England but with two Tests for Britain *v.* New Zealand to his credit.

The most important change, however, was the recall of Burland who, with two penalties, a try and a conversion, scored all England's points in the 11–8 win in Dublin.

Burland, a burly centre who ran straight, gave an immaculate display too against Scotland—it was said that nothing like his hand-offs had been seen at Twickenham since Birkett—and England's 16–3 win was hailed as a victory for the west country, Brown (recalled to full-back), Tanner, Gerrard and Gregory also being in fine form, although two tries by Aarvold, who this season led Durham to their first county final since 1914, must not be forgotten.

As Ireland had beaten Wales, England's win meant that

they shared the 1932 international championship with these two countries—a surprising end to a year that had started disastrously.

The 1933 season opened gloomily with Wales, after twenty-three years of trying, at last gaining their first victory at Twickenham. England should have built up a commanding lead in the early stages, but had only a try by Elliot to show for their efforts at half-time. After the interval the Welsh pack, inspired by their new captain Watcyn Thomas, tamed the English forwards, and a dropped goal and try by Boon gave Wales their historic 7–3 win.

A. S. Roncoroni (Richmond) had come into the England pack as a late replacement for G. P. C. Vallance (Leicester) and played well enough to keep his place throughout the season with the result that poor Vallance, though actually selected, never appeared in an international.

This year, in an abortive attempt to end specialization, the International Board recommended that the first forwards on the spot should be the first down in the scrummage, but this seems to have been more honoured in the breach than in the observance and, for the visit of Ireland, England capped three back-row men in C. L. Troop and E. H. Sadler, both Army, who joined a third member of Hampshire's first championship-winning side (the Navy's N. L. Evans) in the pack, and W. H. Weston, son of a 1901 international and, like his father, Northampton and East Midlands.

D. A. Kendrew, a 1930 Lion at this time playing for the Army and Leicester, was recalled and the remodelled pack were certainly livelier than their predecessors. However, the man of the match was another Army man, also a former Lion—Novis, who, after three years in the wilderness, was brought back on the wing and given the captaincy. His swerve brought him two tries: L. A. Booth, a wing from Headingley, went over in the corner after a resolute sprint; Gadney broke and scored from a loose scrum; Sadler forced through from a line-out and Ireland were outplayed to the tune of 17 points to 6.

However, at Murrayfield Scotland won by a try to nil and went on to win the Triple Crown.

England, Wales and Ireland, with one win apiece, shared second place or the wooden spoon—whichever way one cared to look at it.

Chapter Twelve

Triple Crowns and All Blacks 1934–9

The period from 1934 to the outbreak of war was one of sustained successes for England—Triple Crown in 1934, joint runners-up in 1935, victors over the All Blacks in 1936, Triple Crown in 1937 and joint champions in 1939.

Seven new caps were in the side that opened the 1934 campaign by beating Wales three tries to nil at Cardiff.

Full back was H. G. Owen-Smith, who followed W. H. Milton, F. Mitchell, R. O. Schwarz and R. H. M. Hands by playing Test cricket for South Africa and Rugby for England. He had a remarkable sense of anticipation which enabled him to field the ball on the run, an ability to beat oncoming tacklers and a flair for initiating attacks. His selection was due to his part in the defeat of a fancied Cambridge XV by Oxford, who provided two new caps in the three-quarter line—P. Cranmer, a centre in his first season from school who, according to his great adversary Wilfred Wooller, cut in 'with a glancing dash', and A. L. Warr, a speedy wing who replaced Booth, taken ill the morning of the match. The selection of G. W. C. Meikle, a Waterloo wing, meant that, of the three-quarters, only the sound, fierce-tackling Gerrard had been capped before.

Elliot and Gadney were retained as halves and the latter was given the captaincy.

In the pack Northampton provided R. J. Longland, one of England's greatest props, and J. Dicks, a second-row man. G. G. Gregory (Bristol) remained as hooker and the back row comprised H. A. Fry (Liverpool), P. C. Hordern (Gloucester) and J. McD. Hodgson (Northern). The withdrawal of Kendrew and Webb led to the recall of H. Rew (Army) and the capping of the first man from Metropolitan Police—J. C. Wright.

Meikle beat two Welshman to score in the corner. Cranmer

cut through and put Warr over and, in the second half, Meikle scored his second try after Elliot and Gerrard had beaten the defence. Thus all England's nine points were scored by debutants.

J. W. Forrest (Royal Navy) was recalled to the second row for the trip to Dublin with W. H. Weston (Northampton) coming in as a late replacement for the luckless Hordern. After an Irish try, Cranmer broke and Gerrard carried on a move that led to a try by Fry, a highly effective loose forward who touched down again after Owen-Smith had, typically, fielded an Irish kick and given Forrest a reverse pass. Elliot broke away and Meikle was on hand to take a long pass and score. Two of the three tries were converted by Gregory and England won 13–3.

Booth and Kendrew were fit for the Calcutta Cup match at Twickenham and took their places at wing and prop respectively, while C. F. Slow (Leicester), who had made his name in the Midlands' famous victory over the Third Springboks, came in at stand-off to partner his club and county scrum-half Gadney. Shaw gave Scotland the lead with a try but Gerrard put Meikle over to equalize. With ten minutes left, Booth snapped up a loose ball and swerved inside the full back for the winning try.

The season was a triumph for East Midlands who not only won the county championship—and beat the Barbarians—in 1934, but supplied England with five men—Slow, Gadney, Longland, Dicks and Weston. To Gadney went the still unique honour of captaining his county to the championship and his country to the Triple Crown.

However, Gadney, one of the tall, heavy scrum halves who had come to the fore in an attempt to counter the ever-increasing problem of back row spoiling, was not always easy to play with and gave way to the nippy, elusive J. L. Giles (Coventry) for the first two matches of 1935.

Lancashire, whose brilliant backs won them their first county championship since 1891—before the great split had weakened Rugby Union in the county—provided their centres R. Leyland and J. Heaton, who both helped Liverpool become the leading English provincial university in the 1930s. However, though Booth, Cranmer and these two played in all the matches, the selectors could not decide on the best way to align them and Leyland, twice, and Cranmer, once, were selected on the wing, although Cranmer was restored to centre at half-time in the Irish match!

In fact selection policy was difficult to follow in 1935, P. L. Candler, a Cambridge centre, playing fly half in the first match, J. A. Tallent, a Blackheath centre, in the second and J. R. Auty (Headingley) in the third. The pack was more stable, with the Northampton trio of Longland, Dicks and Weston playing in all the games, together with new caps in E. S. Nicholson, the Oxford hooker, A. Clarke, a giant Coventry second row, and A. G. Cridlan, a Blackheath wing forward. Kendrew, who led Eastern Counties to their first county semi-final in 1935 and started the season as England's captain, was kept out of the last match by injury. The lock position was occupied first by D. T. Kemp (Blackheath) and then by A. T. Payne (Bristol).

But the man of the season proved to be Gloucester's H. Boughton who had not appeared in a trial that season—or since 1929. In addition to being a sound full back, his accurate place kicking saved the Welsh match and won the Irish.

A star-studded Welsh side were leading by a Wooller try when Boughton made the score 3–3 with a penalty. His conversion of a try by Giles gave England a 5–3 lead over Ireland which he made 14–3 with three penalty goals in the last twenty minutes.

At Murrayfield, Cranmer dropped a goal but Fyfe converted two tries to make the half time score 10–4 to Scotland and all England had to show for their second half efforts was a try by Booth after a change of direction by Cranmer.

Victory in this match would have given England the 1935 international championship, but they had to be content to share second place (with Wales) to Ireland—whose title was long overdue as their last had been back in 1899!

The 4th of January 1936 was perhaps the greatest day in England's rugby history. Before 72,000 at Twickenham, New Zealand, in the last match of their tour, were beaten 13–0, the only defeat they suffered on English soil until 1972 and still the biggest margin any European country—Lions included—has had over the All Blacks. The teams were:

England: H. G. Owen-Smith (St Mary's Hospital); A. Obolensky (Oxford), P. Cranmer (Richmond), R. A. Gerrard

(Bath), H. S. Sever (Sale); P. L. Candler (St Bart's Hospital), B. C. Gadney (Leicester, capt.); D. A. Kendrew (Army and Leicester), E. S. Nicholson (Leicester), R. J. Longland (Northampton), A. Clarke (Coventry), C. Webb (Devonport Services), W. H. Weston (Northampton), P. E. Dunkley, E. A. Hamilton-Hill (both Harlequins).

New Zealand: G. Gilbert; N. Ball, C. J. Oliver, N. A. Mitchell; T. H. C. Caughey, E. W. Tindill; M. M. N. Corner; J. Hore, W. E. Hadley, A. Lambourn, H. F. McLean, J. E. Manchester (capt.), R. R. King, S. T. Reid, A. Mahoney.

Owen-Smith was back at full back, although this season it was as a centre that he helped Hampshire to its second championship and St Mary's to a hat-trick of Hospitals Cups.

Cranmer and Gerrard remained to provide dash and solidarity in the centre, but there were two new wings in Obolensky, a nineteen-year-old Russian prince who had played for Notts., Lincs. and Derby while still at Trent College and ran as gracefully as an antelope, and Sever, who had been to a soccer school (Shrewsbury) and specialized in crashing through.

Candler, with his ability to take passes above his head or at his ankles, regardless of fast open-side wing forwards coming hard at him, was criticized for not opening up the game like a Stoop or a Kittermaster, but they did not have his problems, and he was the man to partner Gadney.

The front row of Kendrew, Nicholson and Longland and the second row of Webb and Clarke proved such a strong and heavy 'front five' that for once England could take on tourists up front. They even took scrums instead of lines-out.

The pack was locked by the Harlequins captain, Dunkley, recalled after five years, and flanked by the experienced Weston and the new cap Hamilton-Hill.

New Zealand, who had lost twice—to Swansea (11–3) and Wales (13–12)—won the toss and played with the wind.

England were magnificent. The All Blacks started by concentrating on midfield attack. Hamilton-Hill, Candler, Cranmer and Gerrard had been picked to stop them and they did. When they resorted to grub kicks or short punts over the heads of the English backs, Owen-Smith, Candler, Gadney or Obolensky were always in position to deal with them.

Weston policed the blind side in accomplished fashion and

Gadney was here, there and everywhere, saving his side with well judged kicking or stemming a rush by going down to the ball without hesitation. Dunkley led his pack admirably and a report in the *New Zealand Herald* significantly commented on 'England's superiority in the rucks'—a term then unknown in British rugby.

With the sting taken out of the New Zealand attack, the next problem was for England to score. From a scrum Gadney set his backs going and perfectly timed passing gave Obolensky the chance of a run down the right wing. He rounded the full back by lengthening his stride and touched down by the posts. The conversion hit the bar. Two minutes from half-time Cranmer received in loose play, ran powerfully for thirty yards and passed infield to Candler. Obolensky dashed inwards from his own wing, took Candler's pass, flashed through a gap and went over on the left for one of England's greatest tries.

England took charge of the game in the last half-hour. Cranmer side-stepped Caughey and dropped a goal and then again smashed through the New Zealand centre to make an opening for Sever, who took a difficult pass well and made the final score England 13, New Zealand 0.

The rest of the season was anti-climax—especially the next match at Swansea where the two countries who had just beaten the Third All Blacks were expected to produce an epic encounter but only managed a poor pointless draw. In Dublin Sever forced his way over in the corner but Ireland replied with two tries and won 6–3.

Though the backs frittered away many chances in these two matches, they played together throughout the season and it was the forwards who took the blame. For the Calcutta Cup game at Twickenham, H. B. Toft, a brilliant hooker from Waterloo, Dicks, as prop, and R. Bolton and P. W. P. Brook were introduced. The selection of the two last named meant that Harlequins supplied four men to England's back row in 1936!

Bolton crossed after a run by Sever; Candler scored with a dummy and hand-off; Cranmer kicked ahead and beat the Scots to the touch down and England won 9–8 to give them third place in the championship, a disappointing end to a season that had started so well.

However, luck was certainly on England's side in 1937 when

they won their eleventh Triple Crown by scoring a mere 19 points (10 of them by Sever) to their opponents' 14.

Gadney, who had taken a British team to Argentina in the summer of 1936, was short of match practice in 1937 and the captaincy was given to Owen-Smith.

For the first two matches the halves were T. A. Kemp (Cambridge) and Giles. Candler was moved to centre with Cranmer. Sever remained on the left wing but Obolensky had proved a one-season—or more accurately a one-match—phenomenon and never played for England again.

The English pack always held its own. Ever present were Longland and Toft in the front row, Arthur Wheatley (Coventry) and T. F. Huskisson (Old Merchant Taylors) in the second and Weston on the blind side.

R. E. Prescott, a Harlequins prop who later became R.F.U. Secretary, played in the first match instead of the selected Harold Wheatley (Arthur's brother), kept his place for the second but let Harold in for the third when he himself was crocked. D. L. K. Milman (Bedford), an intelligent loose forward, was seriously injured after the Welsh match and D. A. Campbell (Cambridge), J. G. Cook (Bedford), Dicks and Bolton all appeared in the back row during the season and shared in England's remarkable triumph.

Against Wales at Twickenham Giles and Kemp were as good as Tanner and Davies, and Cranmer and Candler as good as Wooller and Davey. Sever, to everyone's surprise, dropped a goal from the Welsh 25 near touch and, as Wales could only reply with a try by Wooller, England won 4–3.

After a pointless first half against Ireland, A. G. Butler, the Harlequins wing, scored a try. Ireland went ahead 8–3 but Cranmer kicked a penalty goal and Sever won the match 9–8 with an unstoppable eighty-yard dash down the left touch-line.

For the Scottish match Gadney was recalled and a new fly-half F. J. Reynolds, the Army and Old Cranleighans, tried. Another soldier, E. J. Unwin (Rosslyn Park), was introduced on the right wing and gave England the lead with a try in the corner. A try by Sever put them six points ahead and there followed heavy Scottish pressure. However, Candler and Cranmer defended magnificently and the Scots' only reply was a penalty goal.

England's 6–3 win was the first time they had not lost at Murrayfield since the ground was opened in 1925 so their Triple Crown triumph in 1937 was very much against the odds.

In 1938 for the first time opponents had to retire ten yards from the place where a penalty was awarded. Previously it was the kicker who in practice had had to retire. As penalties could now be taken nearer the posts, the pundits forecast an increase in penalty goals—and they were right.

At Cardiff Wales and England scored a goal and a try apiece, but Vivian Jenkins landed two penalties and Wales won 14–8.

At Lansdowne Road England, with the wind, led 23–0 at half-time and won 36–14. The Blackheath full back G. W. Parker, whose uncanny sense of position—he never seemed to run after the ball—had helped Gloucestershire win the county championship in 1937, by converting six out of seven tries and landing the inevitable penalty, scored 15 points—equalling the most on debut for England. Reynolds handled, passed and ran magnificently and Oxford's R. M. Marshall was hailed as the new Wakefield. He had all the skills of a second-row forward, yet was also brilliant in the loose. Both Reynolds and Marshall scored tries and Giles, Unwin, Bolton, Prescott and B. E. Nicholson (a Harlequin centre) also crossed.

The Calcutta Cup match saw Scotland, thanks mainly to their fly-half Wilson Shaw, win by two penalties and five tries (21 points) to one dropped goal, three penalties and one try (16) and record their first victory at Twickenham since 1926.

Only seven men—Unwin, Cranmer, Sever, Toft, Longland, Milman and Weston—played in all three matches in 1938 and Cranmer had been dropped after captaining England to their 36–14 victory over Ireland! However, Nicholson, who had played in the first two games, was injured for the Scottish match and Cranmer recalled for his sixteenth successive, and last, international. This was also the last England season for other heroes of the win over the Third All Blacks—Longland (19 caps), Weston (16), Gadney (14), Sever (10) and Candler (10). Unwin, Leyland, Nicholson, Reynolds and Giles, too, had played their last games for England although they all went on the Lions tour of South Africa in 1938 and Giles (as a centre) was a member of the first British side to win a Test there since 1910. It is one of the ironies of Rugby that G. T. Dancer (Bedford) propped in all three Tests, yet was never capped by England.

It was, then, a rebuilt England team that, under the captaincy of Toft, started 1939 by receiving Wales.

Full back was H. D. Freakes, an Oxford South African who had been capped once in 1938. Of the three-quarters, J. Heaton (Waterloo) had played four years before, but the others—wings R. H. Guest (Liverpool University) and R. S. L. Carr (Old Cranleighans) and centre G. E. Hancock (Birkenhead Park)—were new men, as were the halves, G. A. Walker (R.A.F. and Blackheath) and P. Cooke (Richmond). Toft, an expert on hooking and forward play in general, had as props Prescott and D. E. Teden (Richmond). The second row were Harold Wheatley, who assisted Warwickshire to its first championship in 1939, and Huskisson. Marshall was put in the middle of the back row with J. T. W. Berry (Leicester) and J. K. Watkins (Royal Navy and Somerset) as wing forwards.

The pack—intelligent, fast, strong and hard-working—was England's best for years and was kept together all the season. Their superiority won the Welsh match and they were responsible for the only score of the game, Marshall making 20 yards by sheer pace and dash, Watkins dribbling on and Teden getting the touch down.

The same fifteen played against Ireland at Twickenham, but the 5–0 defeat there led to three changes for what was to be the last full international for eight years—Scotland at Murrayfield. E. J. Parsons (R.A.F. and Yorkshire) came in at full-back and T. A. Kemp, captain and stand-off of the St. Mary's team that in 1939 won the Hospitals Cup for a record sixth year in succession, and J. Ellis, a lively player from Wakefield, were the half-backs.

After half an hour Scotland led by two tries to nil but, by the interval, Heaton had equalized with two penalty goals and he won the match 9–6 with his third.

Thus, to the anger of the purists, three penalties beat two tries, and enabled England to share the international championship with Ireland and Wales who had also won two games each and lost one. In fact England reached this exalted position having scored only one try in all their three internationals.

Chapter Thirteen

Post-War Depression 1947–51

The Second World War did not disrupt British Rugby to quite the extent the First had. Inevitably, rugger men were casualties—of those who played for England in 1939 Freakes, Parsons, Cooke, Teden and Marshall were killed in action, while Walker lost an arm—but the war was of a different nature. There were no wholesale losses as there had been on the Western Front from 1914 to 1918, and the necessity to defend Britain meant that there were always plenty of able-bodied men in the country keen to play rugby.

In 1939–40, the winter of the 'phoney war', England, captained by T. A. Kemp, played two Red Cross Internationals against Wales and won both—18–9 at Cardiff and 17–3 at Gloucester.

From 1942 to 1945 'England' played 'Wales' and 'Scotland' twice each season in Services internationals for which Rugby League players were eligible. It is interesting to note that the only man to play for England in all sixteen of these games was the great Northampton tight-head prop Ray Longland who, with his nineteen pre-war caps, could claim to have played in no fewer than thirty-five 'internationals'.

The first post-war season, 1945–6, saw England playing six 'Victory' internationals under Jack Heaton. The first was against the second New Zealand Expeditionary Force (the 'Kiwis'), captained by C. K. Saxton, who lost only to Scotland and Monmouthshire and beat England 18–3. In the other games, England beat Wales 25–13 at Cardiff, Ireland 14–6 at Dublin and Scotland 12–8 at Twickenham, but lost to Wales 0–3 at Twickenham and Scotland 0–27 at Murrayfield.

Thus when the official championship was revived in 1947, though England called on only two men, Heaton and Guest, who had been capped before the war, with a third, Kemp, appearing in 1948, they, and the other countries, had some experienced campaigners available and J. Mycock, in the absence of Heaton, skipper in the first official post-war international (Wales at Cardiff), had fourteen Services and four Victory internationals to his credit. The England team was:

A. Gray (Otley); R. H. Guest (Waterloo), N. O. Bennett, E. K. Scott (both St Mary's Hospital), D. W. Swarbrick (Oxford); N. M. Hall (St Mary's Hospital), W. K. T. Moore (Devonport Services); G. A. Kelly (Bedford), A. P. Henderson (Cambridge), H. Walker (Coventry), J. Mycock (Sale), S. V. Perry (Cambridge), D. F. White (Northampton), B. H. Travers (Oxford), M. R. Steele-Bodger (Cambridge).

England gained a heroic victory. After a quarter of an hour Scott was limping on the wing and Steele-Bodger had been moved into the threes, but the seven English forwards held the Welsh eight and fine tackling upset the Welsh three-quarter line of Ken Jones, Matthews, Cleaver and Les Williams. White gathered a cross-kick by Moore and hurled himself over for a try converted by Gray. Rees Stephens made the half-time score 5–3 and another try gave Wales a one-point lead, but they had held it only a minute before Hall dropped a goal (worth four points up to 1948) to give England a 9–6 win. Hall, a fine kicker whether in defence or to put his side in an attacking position, had a penchant for dropping goals and two drops by him had enabled St Mary's to beat Coventry 8–3 in 1945 and end the Midlanders' run of seventy-two successive victories. In Hall and his centres Scott, a sound player who brought the short diagonal punt to the wing to a fine art, and Bennett, using a body twist to break through, the Hospital had a formidable midfield trio at the end of the war.

However, in Dublin, England were routed 22–0 and the changes for the Scottish match at Twickenham included the introduction of C. B. Holmes, a Manchester winger with an electric burst of speed, as befitted a man who had sprinted for Britain in the Berlin Olympics of 1936 and had set British Empire Games records in both the 100 yards (9·7 seconds) and 220 (21·2 seconds) at Sydney in 1938. Lancashire in 1947 embarked on a hat-trick of county championships and this season supplied England with Heaton (capt.), Guest, Holmes, Mycock and Perry.

Another major influence on England's rugby in 1946–7 was Oxford University, who went to Twickenham unbeaten and defeated Cambridge 15–5. Their captain and scrum half J. O. Newton-Thompson played in the last two internationals and, of his team, Swarbrick, Travers, M. P. Donnelly (better known as a New Zealand Test batsman) and S. C. Newman were capped by England during the season.

Newton-Thompson's long, accurate pass gave Hall room to move against the Scots and England won 24–5. Hall dropped a goal. Holmes streaked away for a try. The thirty-four-year-old Heaton, back as captain twelve years after his first international, converted and also added the extra points to tries by Guest, Henderson and Bennett. The match ended in snow and, as far as could be seen, the players carried one another off the pitch.

This was one of the most severe winters of modern times and for the only time frost caused a Twickenham international to be postponed. The visitors were France who had been restored to the international fold and, as they had resumed their championship in 1942–3, had to be treated very seriously. Bennett cut through and punted ahead for Guest to win the touch down. Jean Prat dropped a penalty goal to equalize and there were only five minutes left when Newton-Thompson broke, made twenty yards and passed to J. George, a second-row man from Falmouth, who scored the winning try.

England thus shared the Five Nations Championship with Wales, but hopes that they would enjoy a post-war boom proved wishful thinking as 1948, 1950 and 1951 saw them holding the wooden spoon.

The 1947–8 season opened with the visit of the 'Third' Wallabies. The 'Second' Wallabies had arrived in 1939 only to find a war starting and had returned home without playing a match. A very fit, useful side, when these Australians played England at Twickenham they had beaten Scotland and Ireland but lost to Wales and twice in England—9–8 to Lancashire and Cheshire and 14–8 to London Counties.

The teams for this first post-war international against a touring side were:

England: S. C. Newman (Oxford); R. H. Guest (Waterloo), N. O. Bennett (United Services), E. K. Scott (Redruth, capt.), D. W. Swarbrick (Oxford); T. A. Kemp (Richmond), R. J. P. Madge (Exeter); H. Walker (Coventry), J. H. Keeling (Guy's Hospital), E. Evans (Sale), S. V. Perry (Cambridge), J. Mycock (Sale), B. H. Travers (Oxford), D. B. Vaughan (Devonport Services), M. R. Steele-Bodger (Edinburgh University).

Australia: B. J. C. Piper; A. E. J. Tonkin, T. Allan (capt.), A. K. Walker, J. W. T. MacBride; N. A. Emery, C. T. Burke; N. Shehadie, K. H. Kearney, E. Tweedale, D. F. Kraefft, G. M. Cooke, D. H. Keller, A. J. Buchan, C. J. Windon.

Australia won 11–0. Windon, a magnificent breakaway forward, notched two tries and Walker, who punted ahead in his own half, gathered himself to score another. These Wallabies had a splendid cover defence. They did not have their line crossed in an international in Britain and they hurled Swarbrick into touch in goal when he looked certain to break that record.

The first home international in 1948 promised well—Wales were held to a draw at Twickenham. Newman kicked a penalty after Bleddyn Williams had failed to play the ball with his foot after a tackle (an offence up to 1958) and Ken Jones scored in the corner to equalize. Newman, a long-kicking South African, was injured and the last ten minutes saw back-row forward Travers as emergency full-back proving that he could put theory into practice. His *Let's Talk Rugger* is perhaps the outstanding manual on the game written by an English international—though he was an Australian and in 1950 captained New South Wales to a famous victory over the Lions who had already twice beaten Australia.

Kemp, a clever fly half with a powerful boot, a side-step and a sound defence, whose first cap had been in 1937, was selected against Ireland at Twickenham but cried off and ended an international career spanning twelve seasons. His successor was Coventry's I. Preece, a cool player with excellent hands who timed his passes well and was a master of the grub kick.

A Preece pick-up led to a try by Guest, converted by the new full back R. Uren (Waterloo) who in 1950 helped Cheshire to its first championship. Ireland had equalized by half-time and went ahead with two quick tries by their key men Kyle and

McKay. Guest intercepted, beat the opposition with a typical side-step and ran over fifty yards in a manner that belied his years for a try converted by Uren to make the score 10–11, but Ireland held out and went on to their only Grand Slam.

Madge, a star of the outstanding Exeter side that had lost only two matches in 1945–6, had performed well in his first three internationals but at Murrayfield he was injured after six minutes. Steele-Bodger, a terrier-like wing forward always likely to turn up in needful and unlikely places, proved his versatility by turning scrum half and at times he seemed to be tackling the whole Scottish side. England led by a Uren penalty at half-time, but Scotland regained the Calcutta Cup, 6–3, with two tries.

R. H. G. Weighill (R.A.F.), who had come to the fore as a wing forward in 1944 when a young fighter pilot and is currently R.F.U. Secretary, was given the captaincy against France in Paris where the new caps included Northampton's L. B. Cannell, a classic centre with acceleration and the knack of creating an overlap by making for the outside centre when he was inside centre, and the Wasps' first direct international—P. W. Sykes, a scrum half able to find touch from impossible positions. The changes meant that no back played in all four home internationals in 1948, and, of the forwards, only H. F. Luya (Headingley) and Perry, the second row pair, Walker, prop, and Steele-Bodger, wing forward, lasted the season.

M. F. Turner, a hefty wing from Old Whitgiftians and Blackheath who had, as an uncapped player, shone for the Barbarians in their first match against a touring team (the Australians), shaped well against France, but the side disappointed and England lost 15–0 to finish bottom of the 1948 table with one draw and three defeats.

The melancholy story continued into 1949. Hall, representing the Army—those were the days of National Service—was back at stand-off and given the captaincy. At Cardiff he scored the first 'three-point' dropped goal for England, but the second half was all Wales who won 9–3.

Ireland won 14–5 at Lansdowne Road—England's seventh successive match without victory—and there were six changes for the French match at Twickenham. W. B. Holmes (Cambridge), a steady full-back who died in his native Argentina at the end of the year, the Oxford centres, Cannell and C. B. van Ryneveld, T. W. Price, a Cheltenham prop, G. R. Hosking, a Devonport Services second row, and V. G. Roberts, a rugged wing forward from Penryn, alone kept their places all season.

The captaincy and fly-half berth went to Preece, and at scrum half the quick service of W. K. T. Moore (Leicester) was preferred to the tenacity of G. Rimmer (Waterloo).

Preece drew his man near half-way and enabled Cannell to score a spectacular try, converted by Holmes. Preece then dropped a goal and France were beaten 8–3.

The new-look pack was in fine form and the side was retained en bloc for the Calcutta Cup match.

J. R. C. Matthews, a Harlequins second row, Vaughan and Travers dominated the lines-out. Roberts was at the head in the loose and there were bonuses in the foraging of J. H. Steeds, the Middlesex Hospital hooker, and the all-round qualities of Oxford's J. MacG. Kendall-Carpenter playing at prop, the position from which he earned immortality by a corner-flagging tackle on J. V. Smith who had run from half-way in the last minute of the 1949 Varsity Match, with Oxford leading 3–0.

R. D. Kennedy, a left wing who had represented Rhodesia before playing for Camborne School of Mines, ran with determination to put England 3 points up against Scotland. The long-legged van Ryneveld (later South Africa's cricket captain) added two tries to the two he had scored for Oxford in the 1948 Varsity Match. Vaughan broke from a line out and Hosking bullocked his way through, and Cannell made an opening for Guest who flashed over. England won 19–3 and so finished 1949 joint runners-up to Ireland—a happy note for the thirty-one-year-old Guest to end an England career that had spanned eleven seasons.

However, the gloom returned in 1950 when Wales, under J. A. Gwilliam, gained their second win at Twickenham in forty years before the record crowd for the ground of 75,000—so many could not see the game that subsequently numbers have been restricted.

J. V. Smith, an enterprising wing from Cambridge with a fine turn of speed, intercepted and, from forty yards out, scored what proved to be the only try of the season against Wales. The new full-back M. B. Hofmeyer, an Oxford South African who fielded and kicked superbly, put England 5 points up with his conversion. They led 5–3 at half-time but, after the interval, they were handicapped by injuries to Hosking, their pack leader, and Vaughan, their lock, and Lewis Jones, the new eighteen-year-old Welsh full back, converted a try and landed a penalty. Wales won 11–5 and went on to their first Triple Crown for thirty-nine years.

For the Irish match at Twickenham—won 3–0—Moore was recalled to partner Preece at half, and the pack was remodelled. Kendall-Carpenter and the solid, consistent W. A. Holmes (Nuneaton) were retained as props, H. A. Jones (Barnstaple) in the second row and H. D. Small (Oxford) at wing forward. Steeds (capped from Saracens) was recalled to hook and Matthews into the second row, Coventry's S. J. Adkins was given a first cap at lock, and Roberts was fit to resume at wing forward. Roberts was England's hero as he dashed up outside Smith and took a scoring pass when the winger was tackled.

J. V. Smith had a remarkably successful first, and only, season—he scored four of England's five tries and gave the pass for the fifth—and kept his place throughout 1950, as did the Oxford centres Cannell and B. Boobbyer. On the left wing for the first two matches was Oxford's I. J. Botting, who had toured South Africa with the 1949 All Blacks, but he was replaced by Northampton's J. P. Hyde, who the previous season had played in the first of the English Schools '19 group' internationals.

In Paris Smith followed up a punt by Preece to equalize, but France scored a second try and won 6–3.

At Murrayfield Smith again made the score 3–3 with a try. Scotland led 8–3 at the interval, but Hofmeyer landed a penalty, and converted a second try by Smith, after a kick deep towards the corner by Cannell, to put England 11–8 up. However, Scotland fought back with a try and Gray's conversion gave them the match 13–11—and England the wooden spoon.

It was, therefore, hardly surprising that England had only three representatives in the first post-war Lions side—to New Zealand and Australia in 1950. They were Preece (their captain), Rimmer and Roberts, called in when the originally selected J. R. C. Matthews withdrew. Preece, second-string fly half to the genius Kyle, had the satisfaction of playing centre in the only Test New Zealand did not win—the 9–9 draw at Dunedin.

1951 was no better for England. Ten new caps—of whom only the wings C. G. Woodruff (Harlequins) and V. R. Tindall (Liverpool University), prop R. V. Stirling (R.A.F. and Leicester) and second row D. T. Wilkins (R.N. and Roundhay) lasted the season—went to Swansea for England's last international there and Wales won 23–5.

Kendall-Carpenter, the new captain, missed the Welsh match but was back in his best position (lock) for the trip to Dublin. His home club was Penzance & Newlyn, formed by amalgamation in 1945, and their J. M. Williams was brought into the centre to partner Preece, moved from fly half to accommodate E. M. P. Hardy. E. Evans (Sale), first capped as a prop in 1948, established a more or less regular place as hooker up to 1958 and B. A. Neale (Rosslyn Park and the Army) came into the second row.

England's performance was better—Ireland only won by a penalty goal to nil—but their fortunes reached their nadir next match. France won in England for the first time after forty-five years' trying. Jean Prat was their hero with a try, a dropped goal and a conversion in their 11–3 victory. England's cause was not helped by injuries to E. N. Hewitt, the Coventry full-back, and G. C. Rittson-Thomas, the Oxford wing forward, which reduced them to six forwards.

East Midlands won the county championship for the second time in 1951 and their captain, open-side wing forward D. F. White (Northampton), and centre A. C. Towell (Bedford) forced their way into the side to play Scotland, both after three years in the international wilderness. Another change saw the introduction of scrum half D. W. Shuttleworth to join his Army, Blackheath and Yorkshire partner Hardy. Hardy was always a source of danger with his sudden breaks and served his centres well. However, the match winner was White whose spoiling tactics were not always popular. Scotland heeled on their line and fumbled. White picked up and dodged over for W. G. Hook, the Gloucester full-back, to convert. Scotland could only reply with a late try in the corner.

England's 5–3 win meant that they shared the wooden spoon with their opponents, but in Stirling, Evans, Holmes, Wilkins, Kendall-Carpenter and White they had the nucleus of a pack that was to ensure a revival in their fortunes.

Chapter Fourteen

Champions Again 1952–5

1951–2 opened with the first tour by the Springboks for twenty years. When they arrived at Twickenham for the international they had beaten Scotland 44–0, Ireland 17–5 and Wales 6–3, but had suffered what was to prove their only defeat in thirty-one matches in Britain and France—11–9 to the following London Counties side:

G. Williams (Llanelly); J. E. Woodward (Wasps), A. E. Agar, H. C. Forbes (both Harlequins), J. Boothman (St. Thomas's Hospital); N. M. Hall (Richmond), P. W. Sykes (Wasps); R. F. Johnson (Metropolitan Police), O. S. Kverndal (Rosslyn Park), J. F. Herbert (Wasps), J. R. C. Matthews (capt.), A. A. Grimsdell (both Harlequins), D. F. Bland (Colchester), P. W. Kininmonth (Richmond), D. S. Gilbert-Smith (London Scottish).

This result, and the success of Middlesex who in 1951 reached the county final for the first time since 1929 and in 1952 won their second championship, had an influence on the selection of the England XV which was:

W. G. Hook (Gloucester); J. E. Woodward (Wasps), A. E. Agar (Harlequins), L. B. Cannell (St. Mary's Hospital), C. E. Winn (Rosslyn Park); N. M. Hall (Richmond, capt.), G. Rimmer (Waterloo); W. A. Holmes (Nuneaton), E. Evans (Sale), R. V. Stirling (R.A.F. and Leicester), J. R. C. Matthews (Harlequins), D. T. Wilkins (U.S., Portsmouth), A. O. Lewis (Bath), J. MacG. Kendall-Carpenter (Penzance and Newlyn), D. F. White (Northampton).

South Africa: J. Buchler; P. Johnstone, R. van Schoor, M. T. Lategan, J. K. Ochse; J. D. Brewis, P. A. du Toit; H. J. Bekker,

W. Delport, A. C. Koch, E. Dinkelmann, J. du Rand, C. J. van Wyk, H. Muller (capt.), S. P. Fry.

South Africa, were run very close. Du Toit slipped over for a try while the English forwards were still pushing and Muller converted. Winn, a wing with an urge to get involved, followed up a missed penalty to snatch a try under the nose of the Springboks and make the half-time score 5–3. The stamina and strength of the English pack stopped the South Africans breaking loose as they had so often on the tour and they only won 8–3, Muller adding a penalty.

England lost a 6-point lead over Wales at Twickenham. Woodward, a wing whose height (6 ft 1 in.) and weight (14 st. 10 lb.) made him difficult to stop, especially when his hand off was working well, picked up, raced away and put in Agar, a sound centre who had joined Harlequins via Durham and Lloyd's Bank, for a try by the posts. The conversion failed, as did that of a try two minutes later by Woodward. Malcolm Thomas, however, converted a try by Ken Jones to make the half-time score 6–5. Jones sped over for the winning try and Wales went on to a Grand Slam.

Owing to the death of King George VI, the Irish match was postponed and the next game was at Murrayfield. England's 19–3 victory marked a turning-point—it was the first of ten successive internationals in the championship without defeat.

Two more Middlesex players—centre B. Boobbyer (Rosslyn Park) and scrum half P. W. Sykes (Wasps)—were brought into the team again and a first cap was given to P. J. Collins, the Camborne full-back. England led by 5 points at the interval, Hall having converted a try scored by Winn after a cross kick by Agar. Three tries came in a brilliant quarter-hour in the second half. Evans scored from a line-out. Winn cut inside and Lewis, an industrious blind side who had been prevented by a war wound from resuming rugger until he was twenty-eight but who had captained Bath to their record season in 1950–1 and won his first cap at the age of thirty-one, sent Woodward in. Boobbyer jinked and dummied his way through and White, backing up, put Kendall-Carpenter over. Scotland scored a try but Agar had the last word with a dropped goal.

Ireland, in the snow at Twickenham, was memorable for an

immaculate display by Collins who handled the slippery ball wonderfully and dropped on fearlessly. Boobbyer, always a man to follow up, got the touch down after a cross kick by White and England won 3–0.

England's first win in Paris since the war gained them second place in the 1952 Five Nations Championship. France scored an early try but Hall landed two penalties to give England a lucky 6–3 victory.

Collins gave a resolute display of tackling in this match, but a knee injury terminated a promising career, and in 1953 the England selectors turned the captain 'Nim' Hall into a full back, and banked on an attacking fly half in M. Regan (Liverpool).

The accent on attack paid off, and England won the international championship outright for the first time since 1937.

At Cardiff, after a Welsh penalty, R. C. Bazley, a swift, deceptive wing from Waterloo, danced round Ken Jones, then went the other way to beat Bleddyn Williams and Cannell moved outside him to score the only try of the match. Hall converted and in the second half Woodward made the score 8–3 with a penalty.

The match in Dublin was hard fought. Regan jinked through the Irish defence and Evans crashed over. In an exciting second half Ireland equalized with a penalty, Hall restored England's lead with a similar score; Ireland went ahead with a try and a penalty and Hall drew the match 9–9 with a forty-yard penalty.

J. Butterfield (Northampton), a centre who was one of the first Loughborough Colleges products to make his mark and this season helped Yorkshire under the England pack leader Wilkins win their first championship for twenty-five years, made an auspicious debut against France at Twickenham. In the first minute he intercepted, and showed both his eye for the gap and his superb timing of a pass to put Woodward over. A forward effort led to a try by Evans, and in the last minute Regan and Butterfield combined for a try by the latter. Hall's conversion made the score 11–0. One astute journalist predicted, 'Butterfield has come to stay.' He had—for twenty-eight successive games, still the record by a back for England, and third only to Wakefield's twenty-nine in a row and Pullin's thirty-six.

For the Scottish match England preferred Yorkshire's Shuttleworth at scrum half to the courageous, resilient Sykes and gave a first cap to a powerful 13½-stone centre—W. P. C. Davies (Harlequins). The side that clinched the first outright championship for sixteen years in fine style was:

N. M. Hall (Richmond, capt.); J. E. Woodward (Wasps), J. Butterfield (Northampton), W. P. C. Davies (Harlequins), R. C. Bazley (Waterloo); M. Regan (Liverpool), D. W. Shuttleworth (Headingley); W. A. Holmes (Nuneaton), E. Evans (Sale), R. V. Stirling (Leicester), S. J. Adkins (Coventry), D. T. Wilkins (U.S.), A. O. Lewis, J. MacG. Kendall-Carpenter (both Bath), D. F. White (Northampton).

Bazley scored two tries and Adkins, whose 6 ft 4½ in. had much to do with England's line-out successes this season, added another before half-time. Stirling, Butterfield and Woodward touched down after the interval. Hall converted four of England's six tries and England won 26–8.

The draw in Dublin in 1953 had stopped England taking the Triple Crown but this was duly won again in 1954.

For the Welsh match at Twickenham I. King (Harrogate), whose attacking play had helped Yorkshire to the championship in 1953, was capped at full back. J. P. Quinn (New Brighton), a centre with a fine burst of speed, replaced the injured Davies—and kept his place for the season. Rimmer, given his Lancashire partner Regan, at last came good as England's scrum half. There were four new caps in the scrum—D. L. Sanders, a prop who had joined Harlequins from Ipswich Y.M.C.A., the second-row men P. G. Yarranton (R.A.F. and Wasps) and P. D. Young (Clifton and Gloucestershire, but at that time playing for Dublin Wanderers) and R. Higgins (Liverpool), a robust blind side. D. S. Wilson (Metropolitan Police), captain of the Middlesex side that won the championship in 1954, established a regular place as an open-side wing forward always up in support and able to handle like a back.

Wilson was in dashing form against Wales and blotted out Cliff Morgan. After a Welsh try, Regan began a move carried on by Butterfield and Woodward equalized with an irresistible dash for the corner. Woodward again pounded over early in the second half, but with three minutes to go Wales equalized with a penalty. Incredibly, England came back. Regan slid away; Evans, Wilson and Quinn made ground before Kendall-Carpenter threw an overhead pass to Winn who went for the corner and snatched a 9–6 victory.

The first post-war All Blacks side were touring Britain in 1953–4. For once they met an England team that had already played a match and indeed beaten Wales after they had conquered New Zealand 13–8. The teams for the international at Twickenham were:

England: I. King (Harrogate); J. E. Woodward (Wasps), J. Butterfield (Northampton), J. P. Quinn (New Brighton), W. P. C. Davies (Harlequins); M. Regan (Liverpool), G. Rimmer (Waterloo); R. V. Stirling (Wasps, capt.), E. Evans (Sale), D. L. Sanders (Harlequins), P. G. Yarranton (Wasps), P. D. Young (Wanderers), R. Higgins (Liverpool), J. MacG. Kendall-Carpenter (Bath), D. S. Wilson (Metropolitan Police).

New Zealand: R. W. H. Scott; M. J. Dixon, C. J. Loader, R. A. Jarden; D. D. Wilson, L. S. Haig; K. R. Davis; K. L. Skinner, R. C. Hemi, H. L. White, R. A. White, G. N. Dalzell, P. F. H. Jones, R. C. Stuart (capt.), W. H. Clark.

Alas, England's confidence proved misplaced! Apart from some runs by Woodward, England spent most of the game on the defensive and New Zealand won 5–0, Scott, an outstanding full back, converting a try scored by Dalzell.

However, brilliant back play against Ireland at Twickenham led to tries by Regan and Butterfield. King kicked a penalty and Wilson crowned a fine performance with a try. King's conversion made the score 14–3.

There were four new caps against Scotland at Murrayfield—N. Gibbs (Harlequins), full back; E. Robinson (Coventry), hooker; J. F. Bance (Bedford), second row; and V. H. Leadbetter (Edinburgh Wanderers), lock.

Strong runs by Quinn led to England's first two tries—by Young and Wilson, Gibbs converting both. Scotland replied with a try but Wilson romped over for his second. England's 13–3 victory meant that they had won the Triple Crown at last.

Unfortunately, that excellent prop Bob Stirling could not end his career by leading England to a Grand Slam at the age of thirty-four; France, who had beaten the All Blacks, won

11–3 in Paris, Wilson obtaining his fourth try of the season for England. As Wales had beaten France, England and these countries were joint champions in 1954.

Loss of form and illness meant that, of the side that had won the Triple Crown so well in 1954, only Butterfield, Davies, Higgins and Young, who finished as captain, survived to play in all the 1955 matches.

Hall was recalled as full back and captain for the first two internationals and equalled Wakefield's record of having skippered England thirteen times. His rugger career, like his life, saw more ups and downs than most, but he had had the distinction of leading England to the championship in 1953.

D. G. S. Baker (Old Merchant Taylors) and J. E. Williams (Old Milhillians), a well built pair of halves who had helped Middlesex win another county championship in 1954, played in all four games, as did the new front row of D. St G. Hazell (Leicester), N. A. Labuschagne (Guy's Hospital) and G. W. Hastings (Gloucester). J. H. Hancock (Newport), second row, P. J. Taylor (Northampton), lock, and P. H. Ryan (Richmond), open side, appeared against Wales and Ireland but were replaced for the French and Scottish games by Yarranton, I. D. S. Beer (Old Whitgiftians and Harlequins) and Wilson, fit after jaundice. The selection of Butterfield, Hazell and Taylor meant that three former Loughborough students played in the same team.

Wales were met in a typical Cardiff mud-bath and the only score was a Welsh penalty after ten minutes. Baker, tackling hard, stopping rushes and using his height and weight to burst up field, looked the best of England's new caps.

In Dublin England started well with tries by Butterfield and Hastings in the first ten minutes, but they faded and Ireland drew 6–6.

England again had a 6-point lead against France at Twickenham, Hazell kicking a penalty and Higgins crashing over after F. D. Sykes, the new winger from Northampton, and Yorkshire (for whom he made seventy-nine appearances), had turned inside. However, Prat dropped a goal and Vannier converted a try to put France ahead 8–6. Hazell nudged England into the lead with a penalty from fifty-five yards, but in the last ten minutes France won the match 16–9 with another converted try and another Prat dropped goal.

The Calcutta Cup match at Twickenham was nearly the same story. England led 9–3 at the interval through a penalty by Hazell and corner tries by Sykes and Beer. Scotland attacked most of the second half but could only muster a try. England's 9–6 win meant that they finished fourth in the championship.

N. S. D. Estcourt, a Rhodesian full back playing for Blackheath, and Labuschagne, a former Western Province hooker at Guy's, played against Scotland and became the last in a long line of what had once been termed 'colonials' to represent England. Most of them were students and they included such illustrious players as the Australians Wade, Brown and Travers and the South Africans Mellish, Black, Owen-Smith and van Ryneveld.

The strengths and weakness of England's Rugby at this time were reflected in the selection of the Lions party to tour South Africa in 1955. Three of the centres (Butterfield, Davies and Quinn) were English as were two of the scrum halves (Williams and the uncapped R. E. G. Jeeps), a fly half (Baker) and a wing (Sykes). Higgins and Wilson, the wing forwards, went, but not one front or second row.

Winning the First Test 23–22 and the Third 9–6, the British side drew the series two-all and were the most successful Lions to visit South Africa this century until the 1974 team. Butterfield and Davies returned with the reputation of being the best British centres to tour there. Jeeps played in four Tests before representing England. Baker was full back in the vital third Test when all the Lions' points came from Englishmen, Butterfield scoring a try and dropping a goal and Baker kicking a penalty.

Higgins did not play after being injured in the First Test and missed the 1955–6 home season, but England discovered some first-class forwards and a magnificent leader.

Chapter Fifteen

Winning under Evans 1956–8

In 1956 H. C. Catcheside and his fellow selectors recalled the veteran hooker Eric Evans, who in the final trial had led the Rest to a 20–3 victory over England, and gave him the England captaincy. Evans represented Lancashire on 117 occasions, and in 1955 had led them to win the county championship. He now welded the national side into a team both on and off the field by keeping them together from the time they assembled to the time they dispersed.

A great tactician who studied the opposition—and the referee—carefully, Evans's pre-match chats were masterpieces of down-to-earth rhetoric and he was for ever encouraging his players individually as he passed them on the field of play, where he set a fine example by his own work rate. A fitness fanatic, he was thirty-seven when he laid down the captaincy with the record of nine wins, two draws and two losses, second in terms of success only to the immortal W. J. A. Davies, under whom England played eleven, won ten and drew one.

His first match as skipper was not auspicious. He was given ten new caps to face Wales at Twickenham—and England lost 3–8.

M. J. K. Smith, later England's cricket captain, had made his name this season with his switch tactics at Oxford but his scrum half, Brace, was on the Welsh side; Smith and Jeeps, fresh from his Lions triumphs in South Africa, were made scapegoats for the English defeat. Regan, with his jinks and side steps so reminiscent of a typical Welsh out half, and Williams, a strong, running scrum half with a genuine reverse pass, were recalled to replace them.

Cannell, too, was recalled for the last three internationals, while Butterfield and the new wings P. B. Jackson (Coventry) and P. H. Thompson (Headingley) played throughout the season as did the new full back, D. F. Allison (Coventry).

The pack, five of them newcomers, stayed together for all four matches. It was D. L. Sanders (Harlequins), E. Evans (Sale), C. R. Jacobs (Northampton), R. W. D. Marques (Cambridge), J. D. Currie (Oxford), V. G. Roberts (Harlequins), A. Ashcroft (Waterloo), P. G. D. Robbins (Oxford).

Against Ireland at Twickenham England led by an Allison penalty at half time and, after the interval, Butterfield sent Jackson over. Evans scored a captain's try which Currie converted. Thompson opened the way for a try by Butterfield via Roberts, an intelligent user of the ball, recalled in 1956 at the age of thirty-one to stand in for the injured Higgins, and two penalties by Currie made the final score 20–0.

Currie's goal kicking won the Calcutta Cup at Murrayfield. He landed two penalties from near touch and converted a corner try by Williams, who flashed over after a typical blind-side break. England won 11–6.

In Paris England had to beat France to share the championship with Wales, but they were never in the lead. Thompson crossed after a run by Cannell to equalize a French penalty. Allison kicked a penalty after the French had gone ahead 6–3 and another after France had scored two tries, one converted.

The result—14–9 to France—meant that England were joint runners-up in 1956 but 1957 saw their promise fulfilled.

They completed the Grand Slam for the first time since 1928—and the only time since the Second World War.

The seventeen players who brought about this feat are worthy of detailed attention.

The original full back was Allison, slight in build but a sound tackler. He was a perfect catcher of the ball, aided if conditions required them by mittens, and an accurate line-kicker. He had to cry off through injury and full back in the last three games was R. Challis (Bristol), an adventurous player, strong under pressure, who sometimes placed his penalty kicks for touch.

On the right wing was Jackson—a genius who could ghost his way through any defence. Amongst his many gifts were a devastating sidestep that made opponents appear to mistime their tackles hopelessly, a dummy kick-ahead that more often than not saw his marker turn round to chase a ball that was still in the wing's hands and a facility for keeping pace in reserve to beat a man.

On the left was Thompson, a tall, attacking wing whose long legs, hand off and willingness to drop his shoulder and drive through made him difficult to stop once he was in his stride.

Centre all the time was the admirable Butterfield, at this time at his peak. Perfectly balanced, he ran with the ball in front of him in both hands so that he could either give a model pass for the receiver to run on to or use the ball to effect a break through by means of a dummy. Butterfield had a wonderful sense of timing in everything he did—including a tackle that took both man and ball out of the game.

Cannell, in his prime perhaps the fastest of England's post-war centres, was centre the first two games and brought his caps to nineteen, spread over ten seasons. He was at St Mary's, and the last man capped direct from Hospitals rugger, once so powerful. He retained his speed from a standing start and his phenomonal change of pace, but for the French and Scottish games made way for the enigmatic W. P. C. Davies (Harlequins), whose speed and weight made him a world-beater on his day but who was always liable to lapses when taking or giving passes. In fact Butterfield and Davies, so brilliant a pair in South Africa, only played together in the England centre on nine occasions.

The new fly half was the Harlequins captain R. M. Bartlett, who had won a Blue at Cambridge in 1951. He was a fine distributor of the ball, a precise kicker, able to land the ball exactly where it was wanted, and a good tackler—a bonus in an age when many fly halves left tackling to their open side wing forwards. Bartlett never played for a losing England team.

R. E. G. Jeeps, the india-rubber man from Northampton, at last established a regular place at scrum half. His pass was not long but he knew when to feed the ball and when to protect his stand-off. No one has surpassed his ability to clear up and he established a fine understanding with his back row in both defence and attack.

His back row in 1957 were Robbins, Ashcroft and Higgins.

Robbins was an amazing handler of the ball and his ability to pick up in the loose and set up an attack made him the 'father' of second-phase play. Quick off the mark and superbly fit, he liked to stay on his feet to force opposing backs across the field or to cover behind in defence.

The solid Higgins took a lot of stopping and his defence was such that even Cliff Morgan did not use the blind side against him because he knew that Higgins would not buy his dummy or side-step. Ashcroft was a strong man and good tactician at 'Number 8' as the 'lock' position was now called.

The second-row pair—or 'locks' as they can now be called—were Marques (6 ft 5 in. and 15 st. 12 lb.) and Currie (6 ft. 3 in. and 15 st.). Currie was the more powerful—if he went, he really used his weight—and was usually at number 3 in the lines-out for the low trajectory throw. Marques, the more mobile, liked the ball high at number 5. They formed a partnership that represented England for twenty-two successive internationals, and their two-handed catching gave England such superiority in the lines-out that opponents resorted to tapping back.

Propping Evans were G. W. Hastings (Gloucester), a loose-head with an acute positional sense, first capped in 1955 and recalled when Sanders was injured in a road accident, and Jacobs, an intelligent tight-head who could not be pushed back when he had driven over a ball and whose long arms made him adept at turning a man in a standing ruck.

The Welsh hurdle at Cardiff was overcome by a penalty kicked by Allison after Ashcroft had made a dash down the touch line. From the line-out ten yards from his line, a Welsh winger strayed offside near his own posts and that was that.

The Irish match resulted in England's first win in Dublin since 1938 and was achieved with 14 men, Thompson going off with a rib injury after twenty-five minutes. Ashcroft went on the wing, but the seven forwards rose to the occasion. Jackson fielded an Irish kick that had missed touch and beat two or three defenders to score one of his 'impossible' tries, and Challis, who had never wilted under a barrage of garryowens, made the final score 6–0 with a penalty.

Jeeps excelled against France in the Twickenham mud. Thompson carved his way through the middle before passing to Butterfield and Davies let Jackson have the ball with two opponents to beat—which he did to score wide out. After a half-break by Bartlett, Jackson made the half-time score 6–0 with his second try. After the interval France came back with a try converted by Vannier, but the England forwards took charge and Evans himself touched down to give England a 9–5 victory.

The Calcutta Cup match at Twickenham was a tremendous battle. Butterfield broke through and sent Davies over and Challis landed a penalty, but, with twelve minutes to go, England's lead was only 6–3. At this stage Higgins broke away and sent Thompson in, and Higgins, playing the game of his life, then charged through the Scots to score himself. Challis converted both the second-half tries. England had won 16–3 and taken their total of Grand Slams to a record seven. Wales equalled this number in 1976, and surpassed it in 1978, but France have only two to their credit (1968 and 1977) and Scotland (1925) and Ireland (1948) one each.

The championship was retained in 1958. There were only two new caps for the Welsh match at Twickenham—at fly half, the left-footed J. P. Horrocks-Taylor (Cambridge), who specialized in the high kick for forwards to run on to and proved an enigma at international level, and R. E. Syrett, a quicksilver wing forward from Wasps, adept at picking up the loose ball and using it.

Wales took a shock lead with a penalty by T. E. Davies and it was ten minutes after the interval before Butterfield streaked through and Robbins, England's best forward, showed his skill by giving Thompson a chance to dive over wide out for the only try of the match which was drawn 3–3.

The next match was against the Fourth Wallabies who, losing fifteen games including all five internationals, proved the least successful of the major touring sides to visit Britain and France, although they came very close to victory over England at Twickenham. The teams were:

England: J. G. G. Hetherington (Northampton); P. B. Jackson (Coventry), J. Butterfield (Northampton), M. S. Phillips (Oxford), P. H. Thompson (Headingley); J. P. Horrocks-Taylor (Cambridge), R. E. G. Jeeps (Northampton); G. W. Hastings (Gloucester), E. Evans (Sale, capt.), C. R. Jacobs (Northampton), J. D. Currie (Oxford), R. W. D. Marques (Cambridge), R. E. Syrett (Wasps), A. Ashcroft (Waterloo), P. G. D. Robbins (Oxford).

Australia: T. G. Curley; R. Phelps, S. W. White, J. K. Lenehan,

K. J. Donald; A. J. Summons, D. M. Connor; G. N. Vaughan, J. V. Brown, R. A. L. Davidson (capt.), A. R. Miller, D. M. Emanuel, N. M. Hughes, K. J. Ryan, P. T. Fenwicke.

These Australians had to play all out to hold their own and one or two of them were fond of tackling late. Horrocks-Taylor went off with a leg injury after twenty-five minutes, Butterfield going fly-half and Robbins centre. Butterfield was laid out three times and the new full-back Hetherington, who admittedly brought a lot of trouble onto himself by his habits of crash tackling head on and of trying to run through opponents, was so badly concussed that he collapsed at no side and had to be carried off.

Australia led at half-time thanks to a penalty from near touch by the unpopular Lenehan. The new centre Phillips, well served by Robbins who could draw a man and make a half-break as well as anyone, made an outside break to score wide out and equalize. Curley dropped a goal and with one minute of ordinary time left Australia were still leading 6–3. However, Hetherington made the scores level again with a penalty ten yards from touch and, when Butterfield was knocked out for the third time, Evans on his thirty-seventh birthday and playing against a touring side for a record fourth time, had given the order 'shit or bust'. In the sixth minute of injury time the inimitable Jackson gained possession thirty-five yards out and miraculously beat three opponents to score in the corner and gain an epic 9–6 victory for England.

Against Ireland at Twickenham England established an early lead of 6 points through a penalty by Hetherington and a try by Ashcroft and held on to it. This match saw Kyle, the great Irish fly half, set a new British record by gaining his forty-fifth cap; he played once more for Ireland and his forty-six caps have only been surpassed by Kiernan, McBride and Gibson (Ireland), Carmichael (Scotland) and Edwards Wales).

There was a decisive 14–0 win over France in Paris. Bartlett, recalled to fly half for the last three internationals, punted ahead, accurately as usual, Butterfield picked up and Thompson scored a try converted by Hastings. After a break by Phillips, Thompson crashed over and Jackson scored a glorious try from half-way. Hastings completed the scoring with a penalty, and the crowd bayed for the heads of the French selectors.

A. J. Herbert (Wasps), a splendid handler, tackler and coverer, had come in as wing forward against France and kept his place for the Calcutta Cup match at Murrayfield where Allison, who had led Warwickshire to the first of their seven county championships in eight seasons, reappeared at full back.

The game was a disappointing 3–3 draw—a penalty goal apiece—but England's two wins and two draws were sufficient for them to retain the Five Nations Championship, and the remarkable Evans retired with thirty caps to his credit, only one short of the then England record of thirty-one, held by the great Wakefield himself.

Chapter Sixteen

More Championships 1959–63

In 1958–9 the first of the modern laws designed to make the game more flowing were introduced. Instead of having to play the ball with the foot after a tackle, players could pick it up straight away. Instead of having to kick penalties at least five yards in the direction of the opponents' line, the short penalty in any direction was permitted, although the kicker could not yet tap the ball to himself. The quaint custom of requiring a man (usually the scrum half) to place the ball for conversions was abolished and kicks at goal after tries could be both placed and kicked by the kicker. This made goal kicking much easier, especially in representative matches where having a strange placer could be a distinct disadvantage to a kicker.

With a faster game, and more conversions, many clubs scored more points than ever before, but the international scene was still bogged down by the defences and England's four games produced only 9 points for (all penalties!) and 11 against (a goal and two penalties).

The goal against was a try by Bebb converted by Terry Davies in the Cardiff mud and gave Wales a 5–0 victory. In Dublin England won by a penalty goal to nil. The French and Scottish games were both 3–3 draws—a penalty apiece. England's four points from four games made them joint runners-up to France who, with five points, won the Five Nations Championship for the first time.

In an endeavour to exploit the law changes, England went for mobile ball-handing props in G. J. Bendon (Wasps) and L. H. Webb (Bedford), both of whom had started life as wing forwards. The hooking duties were shared by J. A. S. Wackett (Rosslyn Park) and H. Godwin (Coventry) and the season finished with a back row of Herbert, Ashcroft and

J. W. Clements, the Old Cranleighans' captain and the last man to be capped directly from an old boys club.

The old firm of Marques and Currie played in all matches, as did full back Hetherington and the three-quarter line that had won the championship the previous year.

However, the halves were new. S. R. Smith, the Cambridge scrum half, had a long service and could break occasionally. His partner was A. B. W. Risman (Manchester University), a complete fly-half who was a deceptive side-stepping runner with both an inside and outside break, yet also distributed the ball with judgment.

For one reason or another Risman only played fly-half for England six times before following in the footsteps of his illustrious father 'Gus' (a former captain of Great Britain's Rugby League XIII) and turning professional. His best Rugby Union was played as the twenty-one-year-old 'baby' of the 1959 Lions party in New Zealand when his blind-side try in the Fourth Test at Auckland brought the British Isles a 9–6 win—only the second British Test victory in the country. The Lions' first try had been a typical Jackson effort—one of the sixteen he scored in New Zealand. England's other representatives on this tour were J. R. C. Young, J. Butterfield, R. E. G. Jeeps, R. W. D. Marques and A. Ashcroft, with J. P. Horrocks-Taylor and W. M. Patterson being flown out as reinforcements. P. G. D. Robbins had been selected but had withdrawn after breaking a leg.

For Young (Oxford and Harlequins), an international sprinter, the tour was some compensation for having to withdraw from the 1956 Olympic and 1958 Commonwealth Games teams and in 1960 he was preferred to Jackson on England's right wing.

In 1960, for the only time, only fifteen men were called on by England during the season. They were:

D. Rutherford (Percy Park); J. R. C. Young (Harlequins), M. S. Phillips (Oxford), M. P. Weston (Richmond), J. Roberts (Sale); R. A. W. Sharp (Oxford), R. E. G. Jeeps (Northampton, capt.); C. R. Jacobs (Northampton), S. A. M. Hodgson (Durham City), P. T. Wright (Blackheath), R. W. D. Marques, J. D. Currie (both Harlequins), P. G. D. Robbins (Moseley), W. G. D. Morgan (Durham University), R. E. Syrett (Wasps).

Risman and Webb had been selected for the first match. Both cried off and England did so well—they won the Triple Crown for the fourteenth time (and last so far)—that no changes were made.

There was a new captain, the irrepressible Jeeps, to mastermind the side, and seven new caps. At full back was Rutherford, an accurate kicker of the ball with either foot and with a flair for extricating himself from awkward situations.

Left centre was Weston, who had come to the fore with Durham City and County and kicked precisely in attack and long in defence. Outside him was the canny Roberts, a former Cambridge Blue and captain of Old Milhillians, able to adjust his pace cleverly and swerve inside or outside.

New men in the pack were Hodgson, a hard-working hooker gaining his first cap at thirty-two; Wright, a solid prop; and, at number 8, Morgan, a former Welsh Schoolboy international from Newbridge who covered well and whose height made him useful at the back of the lines-out.

However the new cap who attracted most attention was the six foot, blond stand-off half Sharp, who enjoyed a dream debut against Wales at Twickenham, tearing gaps in the Welsh defence as he flashed past Haydn Morgan on the outside. After a penalty from wide out by Rutherford, Weston broke through to the full back and put Roberts over. Rutherford converted and kicked another penalty before Sharp broke from half-way and a long pass by Weston led to Roberts beating two men and scoring his second try in his first international. Thus England led 14–0 at the interval and, confining Wales to two penalties in the second half, won 14–6.

Also at Twickenham, Ireland led 5–0, Kiernan (making the first of his fifty-four appearances) having converted a try, until a quarter of an hour from the end when Sharp dropped a goal. With five minutes left, Robbins sent Phillips away and when he was blocked he found Marques at his elbow. Marques, once renowned as the perfect gentleman who would never retaliate, had come back from New Zealand a much harder forward, and he crashed over for the winning try. Rutherford converted to make the final score 8–5.

England's progress was checked in Paris. France were leading by a penalty when Hodgson won a strike against the head. Jeeps sent Sharp away with room to move and Weston scored near the posts. The conversion hit an upright so the final score was 3–3. France were enjoying a golden era at this time—they had been outright champions in 1959 and were again in 1961 and 1962, but this result meant that in 1960 they had to share the international championship with England who at Murrayfield beat Scotland.

After a dropped goal by Sharp, Syrett charged down a Scottish kick to score a try and Roberts followed up a kick ahead by Robbins to score another. Rutherford converted both and England led 13–0 after thirteen minutes. Scotland never really recovered and, though they landed three penalties, Rutherford replied with one and converted a try after Phillips had broken and sent Young flying over. The final score was a try for Scotland by A. R. Smith.

England's 21–12 victory meant that the Triple Crown was theirs again and hopes were high that they would open 1961 by registering that elusive initial win over South Africa.

The teams were:

England: D. Rutherford (Percy Park); J. R. C. Young (Harlequins), W. M. Patterson (Sale), M. P. Weston (Richmond), J. Roberts (Sale); A. B. W. Risman (Loughborough Colleges), R. E. G. Jeeps (Northampton, capt.); C. R. Jacobs (Northampton), S. A. M. Hodgson (Durham City), P. T. Wright (Blackheath), R. W. D. Marques (Harlequins), J. D. Currie (Northern), P. G. D. Robbins (Moseley), W. G. D. Morgan (Medicals), L. I. Rimmer (Bath).

South Africa: L. G. Wilson; H. J. van Zyl, A. I. Kirkpatrick, J. L. Gainsford, J. P. Englebrecht; D. A. Stewart, P. de W. Uys; S. P. Kuhn, G. F. Malan, P. S. du Toit, A. S. Malan (capt.), J. T. Claassen, G. H. van Zyl, F. C. du Preez, D. J. Hopwood.

However, these Springboks won all four internationals in Britain, drew with France and lost only one of their thirty-four tour games—to the Barbarians. Against England their pack was magnificent. Hopwood went through like a tank for a try, du Preez (making the first of his record thirty-eight appearances for South Africa) converted and the tourists won 5–0.

This match marked the end of the Marques–Currie partnership as Currie was ill for the Welsh match, after which Marques was dropped.

Bebb scored two first-half tries for Wales and, though Young showed his blinding speed in going over, that was all and England lost 3–6.

The changes for Dublin included a new full back from Oxford—J. G. Willcox, dependable under pressure and noted for his torpedo punts; a new open-side wing forward—the hard-tackling D. P. Rogers (Bedford), winning the first of his thirty-four caps; the recall of Coventry hooker E. Robinson, seven years after his last selection; and the return of Sharp at fly half, Risman moving to centre. Ireland ran up an 11 points lead before England replied with tries by Roberts and Rogers, one converted by Risman, to make the final score 11–8.

There was surface water at Twickenham for the French match. V. S. J. Harding, a mature student at Cambridge, had been brought in to partner the talented R. J. French (St Helens and Leeds University) in the second row and marked his first international by being up for the scoring pass when Weston drew the full back. Willcox converted but France replied with a goal and the match was drawn 5–5.

For the Calcutta Cup match Horrocks-Taylor was back at fly-half, Sharp having pulled a muscle and Risman having joined Leigh. Patterson, a strong fast runner from Sale, who this season led Cheshire to its second county championship, was recalled to centre and joined his county colleague Rimmer (Old Birkonians and Bath) in the national side. Patterson kicked diagonally for Roberts to score and Horrocks-Taylor landed a penalty, England winning 6–0. Scotland's hopes of the Triple Crown were dashed and England finished fourth in the 1961 table.

In 1962 they finished third. P. J. Taylor, the Northampton number 8, was brought back after seven years to lead the pack and a belated first cap was given to P. E. Judd, the Coventry prop who had played in ten trials and was one of the corner-stones of Warwickshire's great pack. New men in the backs were the Cambridge centre M. R. Wade and A. M. Underwood, a product of St Luke's College, Exeter, who was playing centre for Northampton but was turned into a wing by England.

The Welsh match at Twickenham was a pointless draw. Against Ireland (for whom W. J. McBride was making the first of his sixty-three appearances) Sharp was at his best, cutting through like a knife and finding touch with long, raking kicks. He put Wade in for a try, converted it, kicked a penalty from near touch and converted his own try. Roberts dashed away for a try out of nothing and England won 16–0.

However, they crashed 13–0 in Paris, wing forward Crauste obtaining three tries, two converted by Albaladejo, and there were six changes, three of them enforced, for the match at Murrayfield. Warwickshire had won the County Championship and T. A. Pargetter, P. G. D. Robbins (both Coventry) and S. J. Purdy (Rugby) joined Judd in the pack. Willcox and K. J. F. Scotland exchanged penalties in the 3–3 draw.

Jeeps in his twenty-fouth and last game for England—and his thirteenth as captain—was as skilful as ever in defence and was rewarded with selection for his third Lions tour, returning to South Africa in 1962. There he played in all four Tests and brought his Tests for British Isles to the then record thirteen—eight against South Africa, three against New Zealand and two against Australia. Other England players to make the tour were Willcox (top points scorer with 67), Weston, Sharp, Wright, Hodgson, Rogers and J. M. Dee, a Hartlepool Rovers centre, with H. Godwin, the Coventry hooker, and H. J. C. Brown, an R.A.F. and Blackheath centre who never played for England, going out as replacements.

Sharp had his cheekbone fractured before the first Test, which was drawn 3–3, England supplying Willcox, Weston, Jeeps and Rogers to the side, but the remaining three Tests were lost and few players returned with enhanced reputations.

Fortunately, Richard Sharp was fit for the 1963 internationals and, under his captaincy, England won the international championship outright for the seventeenth time—and the last so far.

The campaign opened with a 13–6 win over Wales at Cardiff. The team that gained this famous victory (England has not won there since) was:

J. G. Willcox (Oxford); P. B. Jackson (Coventry), M. S. Phillips (Fylde), M. P. Weston (Durham City), J. Roberts (Sale); R. A. W. Sharp (Wasps, capt.), S. J. S. Clarke (Cambridge); N. J. Drake-Lee (Cambridge), J. D. Thorne (Bristol), B. A. Dovey (Rosslyn Park), A. M. Davis (Torquay Athletic), J. E. Owen (Coventry), D. C. Manley (Exeter), B. J. Wightman (Coventry), D. P. Rogers (Bedford).

Of the previous season's pack, only Rogers was retained. Wightman, a hard determined number 8, had played once four years before, but the other six forwards were new caps, two of them—Drake-Lee (loose head) and Davis (a fiery lock)—being only twenty years of age. On the other hand Manley, who in 1957 had assisted Devon to their only title since 1912, was representing England for the first time at the age of thirty. A seventh new cap was Clarke, a live-wire scrum half with a useful pass.

There was a surprise recall for Jackson who, since returning from his triumphant tour with the 1959 Lions, had played only once (and that as a last-minute fill-in), but was now given a full season at the age of thirty-two.

The winter of 1962–3 was the severest of the century, and the Welsh match was 'on ice'. From a line-out just outside England's 25, Roberts, who had already used the ploy twice, threw the ball half-way across the field to Weston at inside centre. Weston passed out to Phillips who did a scissors with Jackson and moved outside the winger. Jackson drew the full back and repassed to Phillips who showed his tremendous pace to score one of England's greatest tries. Sharp converted this try and one scored by Owen after Rogers and Phillips had booted the ball on from half-way. Owen, a lithe, speedy lock and useful handler of the ball, was the kind of forward sought at this time when the English forwards were lying further back at opponents' kick-offs and drop-outs and were expected to take the ball running forward and make ground with their impetus.

A Welsh penalty goal was soon countered by a dropped goal from Sharp and there were only ten minutes left when Wales registered their sole try.

Whenever England have won at Cardiff, they have gone on to top the table and there was disappointment that the Irish match, played in a sea of mud at Dublin, was a pointless draw, England's heroes being Clarke and Willcox who were bravery personified.

The same back division was retained for the season but there were three changes in the pack for the French match at Twickenham, K. J. Wilson (Gloucester), prop, T. A. Pargetter (Coventry), lock, and D. G. Perry (Bedford), number 8 and pack leader, gaining places. France scored an early goal but Willcox won the game 6–5 with two penalties—and ensured that the French hold on the championship, which they had won in 1959, 1961 and 1962 and shared in 1960, was broken at last.

For the Calcutta Cup match Coventry's Godwin and Judd were recalled to the front row—and took six heels against the head. Their inclusion meant that five of the Warwickshire side that, under Jackson, had again won the county championship, represented England in 1963. Scotland were 8–0 up before Jackson evaded four tackles, cross-kicked, gathered the ball himself and gave to the forwards who put Drake-Lee over in the corner, Willcox converting superbly against the wind.

Early in the second half Sharp was worked free when Jackson ran into the fly-half position and took the wing forward's tackle. Instead the ball had gone to Sharp who swept through the Scottish middle, dummied the full-back and scored half way out after a run of forty yards.

Willcox's conversion won the game 10–8—and England were champions again.

Chapter Seventeen

More Lean Years 1963–6

In May 1963, England made history by becoming the first Home Country to tour New Zealand. They went as European champions, but several of the men who had taken them to the title—including Sharp, Willcox and Jackson—were not available.

The captaincy was given to M. P. Weston, the Durham skipper, who, with Jeeps, had been the only Englishman to have played in all four Tests for the 1962 Lions, and there were recalls for thirty-five-year-old F. D. Sykes, the Northampton winger who had gained his two caps eight years before, and C. R. Jacobs, a year younger. Jacobs (who led the pack), Godwin and Judd formed a front row that, in the words of a New Zealand journalist, appeared to 'have been carved out of one block of teak'.

Another veteran in the party was the Northampton and Cornwall full back R. W. Hosen, who was nearly thirty and had been waiting to play for England since his first trial in 1954. His positional sense, his catching and tackling and his long-range kicking, either to touch or at goal, were so impressive that he was the only tourist to be made a Player of the Year by *The Rugby Almanack of New Zealand*, which said that it was 'no exaggeration to record that the comparisons between D. B. Clarke and R. W. Hosen on the two occasions they were in opposition did not by any means favour the big All Black'.

Hosen scored 30 of his side's 45 points in the five games in New Zealand, including 11 in the first match against Wellington when England's 14–9 win proved to be their only victory of the tour.

Inevitably, he was one of the three new caps—J. M. Ranson,

a strong-running winger from Rosslyn Park, and V. R. Marriott, a Harlequin blind-side flanker, were the others—for the First Test at Eden Park, Auckland.

England led 6–0 at half time thanks to two Hosen penalties.

Don Clarke replied with a penalty but Simon Clarke, who on this tour established a reputation as a tenacious, hard working scrum half, exploited the blind side and Ranson scored a try converted by Hosen. With fifty minutes gone, England led 11–3 but the All Blacks pack had the last word. By winning rucks they enabled R. W. Caulton to score two tries. Don Clarke converted both, scored and converted his own try and made the final score 21–11 with a left footed dropped goal.

A week later came the Second Test at Christchurch. The teams were:

New Zealand: D. B. Clarke; R. W. Caulton, I. N. Uttley, D. W. McKay; P. T. Walsh, B. A. Watt; D. M. Connor; W. J. Whineray (capt.), D. Young, I. J. Clarke, C. E. Meads, A. J, Stewart, K. R. Tremain, D. J. Graham, W. J. Nathan.

England: R. W. Hosen; F. D. Sykes (both Northampton). M. S. Phillips (Fylde), M. P. Weston (Durham City, capt.), J. M. Ranson (Rosslyn Park); J. P. Horrocks-Taylor (Leicester), S. J. S. Clarke (Cambridge); C. R. Jacobs (Northampton), H. Godwin, P. E. Judd (both Coventry), A. M. Davis (Torquay Athletic), D. G. Perry (Bedford), V. R. Marriott (Harlequins), B. J. Wightman (Coventry), D. P. Rogers (Bedford).

England's performance was epic and they were unrecognizable as the side of previous tour games.

New Zealand took the lead when Meads rampaged from a line-out near half-way and McKay crossed. Hosen replied with a penalty but a try by Walsh put the All Blacks 6–3 up at the interval.

Early in the game England's young lock Mike Davis dislocated a shoulder and returned with it strapped. He injured it again trying to stop Walsh's try and had a pain-killing injection at half-time. He emerged with one arm hanging limp and, in a display of courage unsurpassed in England's annals, proceeded to outjump the New Zealand line-out specialists by catching the ball one handed.

Eight minutes after half-time England equalized with a try described as the best seen in a Test in New Zealand since that of Ken Jones for the 1950 Lions. Sykes fielded an All Black kick in his own 25 and came infield. The ball reached Ranson who swept past three defenders and, when checked, flipped the ball inside. There was Rogers to catch the ball at his ankles and punt for the corner. Phillips gathered on the bounce and dived over.

England were now on top and, though advantage was not taken of half-breaks by Horrocks-Taylor, there occurred twice the remarkable sight of the New Zealand pack being marched back over its own goal-line for Wightman to touch down a pushover 'try'. However the referee thought otherwise and the scores were still level when five minutes from the end Don Clarke made a mark on half-way. He called up his brother Ian (each was setting a New Zealand record by playing his twenty-fourth game for his country) to place the ball for him and, by a ruse they had perfected, persuaded the Englishmen to charge prematurely. Don, thus presented with a free kick at the goal sixty-three yards away, put the ball over the bar and New Zealand won 9–6.

If New Zealanders claim they were robbed at Cardiff in 1905 (and they still do!) Englishmen can claim they were robbed at Christchurch in 1963. Nevertheless their feat there was the best by any British team (Lions and Wales included) in New Zealand in the 1960s.

This tour was far too condensed—England played six matches, three of them Tests, in eighteen days—and three days later the tourists found themselves in Sydney playing Australia. They gave a lethargic display on a water-logged pitch and Australia, who under J. Thornett were embarking on a golden era, won 18–9. This incidentally was the only Test for which J. E. Owen, the Coventry lock, was fit.

In fact England had begun a disastrous period during which they won only two out of seventeen matches.

Most of the players engaged at Christchurch found themselves in opposition again seven months later when the following teams met at Twickenham:

England: J. G. Willcox (Harlequins, capt.); M. S. Phillips (Fylde), M. P. Weston (Durham City), R. D. Sangwin (Hull and East Riding), J. Roberts (Sale); J. P. Horrocks-Taylor (Middlesbrough), S. J. S. Clarke; N. J. Drake-Lee (both Cambridge), H. Godwin, P. E. Judd, J. E. Owen (all Coventry), A. M. Davis (Torquay Athletic), V. R. Marriott (Harlequins), D. G. Perry, D. P. Rogers (both Bedford).

New Zealand: D. B. Clarke; R. W. Caulton, P. F. Little, M. J. Dick; D. A. Arnold, B. A. Watt; K. C. Briscoe; W. J. Whineray (capt.), D. Young, K. F. Gray, C. E. Meads, A. J. Stewart, D. J. Graham, B. J. Lochore, K. R. Tremain.

These Fifth All Blacks lost only to Newport, and at Twickenham won easily 14–0, England's biggest home defeat since the original All Blacks won 15–0 at Crystal Palace five years before Twickenham was opened. Clarke kicked two penalties and Caulton made the score 9–0 with a try after a burst by Tremain. After the interval Meads charged over, Clarke converting with his left foot!

The five changes for the first match of the 1964 international championship—Wales at Twickenham—included the recall of two thirty-five-year-olds—S. A. M. Hodgson, veteran of seventy-five county championship games for Durham, and Jacobs—to the front row and a first cap for thirty-one-year-old Gloucester flanker, P. J. Ford. Ranson celebrated his first appearance for England in Europe with a try in the first minute after a kick ahead by Horrocks-Taylor, who then went round the blind side and enabled Rogers to put Perry over. England were thus 6 points up in as many minutes, but Bebb scored two tries to force a 6–6 draw.

For the Irish match at Twickenham three of the Warwickshire side that had reached the county final again—Jackson, Godwin and the Harlequins lock and captain C. M. Payne—were selected but Jackson cried off and, having led his county to another title, retired with twenty England caps—far fewer than his genius merited. The beaten finalists in 1964 were Lancashire under Phillips, and T. J. Brophy, a Liverpool fly-half at Loughborough Colleges, was brought in against Ireland. A tricky player with a fine pair of hands, his jinks only led to one try and the man of the match, which Ireland won 18–5, was his opposite number, also making his debut—one C. M. H. Gibson.

For the visit to Paris the captaincy was transferred to Jacobs;

there were two new caps in the pack—D. F. B. Wrench, Harlequins, loose head, and T. G. Peart, Hartlepool Rovers, number 8; former Cambridge scrum half S. R. Smith, who had joined Richmond, was recalled after five years, and, controversially, Hosen played on the wing. The changes worked. Godwin took six off the head. Payne and Davis dominated the lines. Ford and Rogers were effective flankers, with the 16½ stone Peart driving foward. Smith's saving kicks were invaluable.

Hosen landed a penalty awarded ten yards from touch, and, after France had equalized with a try, drew the full back before putting Phillips over for England to win 6–3—their last victory at Stade Colombes.

The same side was retained at Murrayfield, but Scotland, with a 15–6 win, regained the Calcutta Cup after fourteen years. This was the last international for Jacobs, whose twenty-nine caps put him next only to Wakefield and Evans, and for Phillips, whose twenty-five appearances for England equal J. D. Currie's record for an Oxford Blue.

England, joint third in the championship in 1964, were fourth in 1965 when there were again major changes in the laws. Scrummage offside lines were created to prevent wing forwards and backs following the ball out and backs, except scrum halves and the thrower-in, had to keep ten yards back at lines-out, the length of which was decided by the side throwing in.

Once again England were slow to profit from law changes, and the meagre 15 points they collected from their four games comprised three penalties and two tries.

A new three-quarter line was thrown into the deep end at Cardiff—almost literally because conditions were atrocious. Three of them—the Oxford wing E. L. Rudd and the Cambridge centres D. W. A. Rosser and G. P. Frankcom—were Oxbridge players and this was about the last time that England selection was influenced by the Varsity match, so long a maker of international players. There was also a disastrous recall, nine years after his last cap, for scrum-half J. E. Williams (Sale). New caps in the pack, each of whom kept his place all season, were N. Silk, the Harlequins blind side, S. B. Richards, the Richmond hooker, and A. L. Horton, a Blackheath tight head, expert in helping his hooker and supporting his line-out men.

Old caps to play in all the matches were Perry (the new captain), number 8, Rogers, open side, Owen, lock, and D. Rutherford, full back of the 1960 Triple Crown side, who had joined Gloucester after training at St Luke's College, Exeter. For the last three matches Judd and Payne, from the Warwickshire XV that was winning its seventh championship in eight years, and Clarke, the Blackheath and former Cambridge scrum half, were recalled.

Wales won 14–3, Ireland won 5–0 and, for the French match at Twickenham, Weston played for England for the first time at stand-off half, the position from which he skippered Durham to the county final in 1965.

The new laws had, presumably, been designed to encourage handling but they also gave kickers more time to perform, and Weston's prodigious efforts in this direction were certainly a factor in England's welcome win. The English forwards were kept going by Perry, the 'gentle giant', who set up attacking moves from number 8, and Richards won ten strikes against the head. Rutherford opened with a penalty. France took the lead with a try and a penalty. Payne equalized by sprinting twenty yards for a try and Rutherford won the game 9–6 with a penalty fifteen yards from touch four minutes from no side.

Neither fly half paid much regard to his three-quarters in the Calcutta Cup match in which there were no fewer than 119 lines-out.

Scotland led by a Chisholm dropped goal when, in the third minute of injury time, the ball went left to the stocky A. W. Hancock, a wing who had recently joined Northampton from Cambridge City and had kept his place after being called in as a late replacement against France. This was about the only time in the match that Hancock received the ball and the Scottish line was ninety yards away. He wriggled out of a tackle and made for half-way, where he stumbled clear of Wilson, the Scots full-back. This left fifty yards to go—and he made the corner to snatch a 3–3 draw from a match that seemed lost.

There was little to enthuse over in 1966 when what was described as 'the poorest England side for years' failed to win a game and finished with the wooden spoon. The selectors' policy was difficult to follow. In the four games they tried no fewer than thirteen new caps including three new scrum halves,

J. Spencer (Harlequins), R. C. Ashby (Wasps) and T. C. Wintle (Northampton), and two new hookers, J. V. Pullin (Bristol) and W. T. Treadwell (Wasps).

Wales won 11–6 at Twickenham, Price kicking two penalties and converting a spectacular try after Pask had dived over, England replying with a Rutherford penalty and a Perry try.

Against Ireland Rogers, the new captain, took the ball on with his feet and J. R. H. Greenwood, a Waterloo blind side, celebrated his debut by going over. Kiernan and Rutherford exchanged penalties but an Irish try ensured a 6–6 draw.

France won 13–0 in Paris, England ending with four players crippled. Among them was Perry, who tore a cartilage after a quarter of an hour and, rather then leave his country short, returned after an injection. His fine gesture ended his rugger career and his fate was instrumental in the decision to allow replacements in internationals two years later.

At Murrayfield the Scottish forwards, inspired by D. M. Rollo, who was on his way to equalling H. F. McLeod's total of forty caps for Scotland, were well on top and England ended a dismal season by losing 3–6.

England's points came from a splendid dropped goal by C. W. McFadyean, a well balanced centre from Moseley, a club that was exploiting the new laws successfully with planned back moves.

McFadyean, Rutherford, Weston and two new caps from Northampton—wing K. F. Savage and prop D. L. Powell—were England's representatives in the 1966 Lions party to New Zealand. They found the All Blacks, under Lochore, at a peak and returned as the only British team to have lost all Tests played in New Zealand. All other Lions teams there—and in South Africa for that matter—have at least scraped one draw in Tests.

Chapter Eighteen

Disciplined Rugby 1967–9

After this disastrous spell, England under a new chairman of selectors, M. R. Steele-Bodger, took the first tentative steps towards organizing the candidates for the national team.

Initially this merely took the form of holding Sunday 'teach-ins' after the trials, but at least an attempt was made to impose a pattern of play, no easy task when Cornishmen and Lancastrians have to be blended with Londoners and Midlanders.

Set moves were practised and policy laid down. From this time onwards team work has become all important, though the insistence on eliminating risks has led to a loss of spontaneity and England were no longer likely to run in many tries from their own 25. Indeed, a preference for playing their Rugby thirty yards from the opponents' line seems to have led to the selection of some backs who are quick over that distance but not necessarily over a hundred yards, and others who might crash through several tackles to get to the line but would be overhauled if left to run a long way.

The first match under the new system was not auspicious. Australia, who, since beating England at Sydney in 1963, had shared a series in South Africa, and beaten New Zealand 20–5 at Wellington and Wales 14–11 at Cardiff, outplayed England to the tune of 23 points to 11 at Twickenham.

The teams were:

England: R. W. Hosen (Bristol); P. B. Glover (R.A.F. Cranwell), C. W. McFadyean (Moseley), C. R. Jennins (Waterloo), K. F. Savage (Northampton); R. A. W. Sharp (Bristol, capt.), R. C. Ashby (Wasps); M. J. Coulman (Moseley), S. B. Richards (Richmond), P. E. Judd (Coventry),

A. M. Davis (U.S. Portsmouth), P. J. Larter (Northampton), J. R. H. Greenwood (Waterloo), G. A. Sheriff (Saracens), D. P. Rogers (Bedford).

Australia: J. K. Lenehan; S. Boyce, R. J. Marks, J. E. Brass, A. M. Cardy; P. F. Hawthorne, K. W. Catchpole (capt.); J. M. Miller, P. G. Johnson, R. B. Prosser, R. G. Teitzel, P. C. Crittle, J. Guerassimoff, G. V. Davis, J. F. O'Gorman.

Brophy had signed for Barrow and Sharp was brought out of semi-retirement and restored to the captaincy, while thirty-three-year-old Hosen was given his first cap as full back in Europe. Though slow about the field, he set new dimensions with his place kicking, collecting 46 points for England during the season, nearly double the previous record of 24, held jointly by D. Lambert, C. N. Lowe and G. W. Parker.

Hosen gave England a 6-point lead with two penalties, but thereafter it was all Australia. Brass and Catchpole scored tries; Lenehan converted one and kicked a penalty, while Hawthorne also landed a penalty and dropped no fewer than three goals. Ashby replied with a try after a neat blind-side break, Hosen converting. The Australian forwards were superb in the loose and from the lines tapped into the incredible hands of Catchpole who, with his partner Hawthorne, was given ample room.

The result was that for the first match in the 1967 championship—Ireland in Dublin—the selectors swept away the entire second and back rows. The only men to retain their places for all five internationals were, in the front row, Judd, given the captaincy, Richards, a 6 ft 2 in. hooker useful in the loose, and Coulman, a tall loose head who was nearly an even-timer; in the three-quarters, McFadyean, a fine support player always on hand for the half-break and likely to beat a man on the outside, and Savage, of above average speed and an intelligent coverer in defence, as wings had become since the 1964 law changes had given halves more time to place their kicks accurately; and, at full back, Hosen.

The new locks were D. E. J. Watt (Bristol), at seventeen stone one of the heaviest men to represent England, and J. Barton (Coventry). Both had good line-out techniques and Barton was a fine handler whose mobility was proved by his two tries, against Wales at the end of the season. J. N. Pallant

(Nottingham) came in at number 8 and the flankers were D. M. Rollitt (Bristol), in attack quick to the break-down and in defence covering behind his backs, and R. B. Taylor (Northampton), a good ball player with a highly developed sense of anticipation.

R. D. A. Pickering (Bradford) was a running scrum half with a short but quick service, always ready to take on the back row and take the pressure off his fly half. His partner was J. F. Finlan (Moseley), a swift mover who revelled in the ten-yard zone at lines-out. His quick passing brought the best out of his three-quarters and his acceleration and dummy could take advantage of a gap.

Glover was injured training for the Irish match and McFadyean was moved on to the wing and the hard tackling R. D. Hearn (Bedford) was brought into the centre.

The result was England's first win over a Home Country for four years, but it was a close thing. With the score a penalty apiece the game entered injury time. Ireland won a line-out just in their own half. Hearn crash tackled his opposing centre. McFadyean, typically, was on the loose ball in a flash, kneed it on, gathered and showed his exceptional speed over thirty yards to score near the posts. Hosen converted with the the last kick of the game.

France had not won at Twickenham for twelve years, but ended the jinx with a 16–12 victory. England rarely looked like scoring a try and were kept in the game by three Hosen penalties and a Finlan dropped goal.

However, England really came good when they regained the Calcutta Cup. Hosen kicked an early penalty, but after half an hour Scotland led 8–3. After good work by Pickering, McFadyean (back at centre) went through on the blind side and Hosen converted. Wilson regained the lead for the Scots with a penalty and again with another after Hosen converted a try by Taylor. Hosen put England 16–14 ahead with his second penalty. Judd, leading by example, and his forwards were scrummaging and rucking effectively and England scored thrice in the last eight minutes. Rollitt and Rogers enabled R. E. Webb (Coventry), a powerful left wing who enjoyed taking people on, to score a try on debut. There followed a superlative try when Finlan intercepted, gave to Hearn, received the ball back and sent McFadyean away for a try converted by Hosen. After a heel against the head Finlan dropped a goal and England had won 27–14. England's 27 points were their most in a match since the 36 scored in Dublin in 1938, and are still the post-war record.

Because of the Australian tour the Welsh match at Cardiff was played in April in perfect conditions. Wales had lost all their four matches but England, having beaten Ireland and Scotland, could win the Triple Crown—and the championship.

Nothing could go wrong for eighteen-year-old Keith Jarrett, who scored 19 points on debut. At the interval Wales led 14–6. England got back in the game at 19–15, but a remarkable try by Jarrett inspired a Welsh burst that took the score to 34–15 before Hosen kicked his fourth penalty and Barton scored his second try. Wales won 34–21 but were left with the wooden spoon, France being champions and England joint runners up.

England's preparations were even more extensive for the next campaign (1967–8). An England XV played three regional fixtures and at the end of September the R.F.U. sent twenty-two players, under the captaincy of Judd, to Canada to mark the Dominion's centenary. All five matches were won easily, 164 points were scored against 9 and, in the representative game at Vancouver, England beat Canada 29–0, Webb scoring four tries.

Ideally the teamwork engendered on such a tour should have served England well during the season, but only eight men who had been to Canada played in the first international versus New Zealand. These All Blacks were on a short fifteen-match tour, and England was divided into three areas to meet them. Their 33–3 win over the North of England in the first match induced a state of panic and, when Midland, London and Home Counties only lost 3–15 after losing Hearn with a dislocated vertebra in the third minute, the selectors decided to base the England team for the big match a week later on that side. Consequently the entire pack, the scrum half and two three-quarters found themselves in the following XV:

D. Rutherford (Gloucester); K. F. Savage (Northampton), C. W. McFadyean (Moseley), R. H. Lloyd (Harlequins), R. E. Webb (Coventry); J. F. Finlan (Moseley), W. J. Gittings (Coventry); A. L. Horton (Blackheath), H. Godwin, P. E. Judd (capt.), J. E. Owen (all Coventry), P. J. Larter, R. B. Taylor (both Northampton), G. A. Sherriff (Saracens), D. P. Rogers (Bedford).

New Zealand: W. F. McCormick; W. M. Birtwistle, W. L. Davis, M. J. Dick; I. R. McRae, E. W. Kirton; C. R. Laidlaw; E. J. Hazlett, B. E. McLeod, B. L. Muller, C. E. Meads, S. C. Strathan, G. C. Williams, B. J. Lochore (capt.), K. R. Tremain.

After thirty-five minutes the All Blacks led 18–0—tries by Kirton (2), Birtwistle and Laidlaw, McCormick converting three—and the game was virtually won. Savage, the blind-side wing, came in on a set move and McFadyean put Lloyd over. Rutherford's conversion made the interval score 18–5 but, with McCormick converting a try by Dick, New Zealand led 23–5. A penalty by Larter and a late try by Lloyd made the final score 23–11.

The All Blacks went on to an unbeaten tour, though in the last match they were given a fright by the Barbarians who were 6–3 up with two minutes to go but lost 6–11.

Lloyd showed his ability as a finisher by scoring the Barbarians' sole try—his fourth in three matches against the Sixth All Blacks—and, with McFadyean (given the captaincy), Savage, Finlan and Larter, kept his place for the first match in the 1968 championship, but otherwise it was back to the drawing-board. Rutherford, one of England's best post-war fullbacks, and Judd, Godwin, Horton and Owen, four of their best forwards, had played their last game for their country.

Only Larter, 6 ft 4½ in., speedy and with good hands, kept his place in the pack. His new partner at lock was even taller—Northampton's M. J. Parsons who had come to the fore in 1965 and 1966 helping Oxfordshire to become the first county in the 'southern' group (created in 1952) to reach the semi-final. The selectors went for height in the back row choosing nineteen-year-old B. R. West (Loughborough Colleges and Northampton), an open side who attacked the fly half, D. J. Gay, the Bath number 8, and P. J. Bell, a blind side from Blackheath who was given the pack leadership on his debut. J. V. Pullin, the Bristol hooker, capped once in 1966, started a run that extended to a record thirty-six successive appearances and was propped by Coulman and a new cap—B. W. Keen (Newcastle University).

Top The first England XV to beat New Zealand—1936. *Standing* (left to right)*:* P. L. Candler, E. S. Nicholson, R. A. Gerrard, E. Hamilton-Hill, A. J. Clarke, A. Obolensky, H. S. Sever, P. E. Dunkley, H. G. Owen-Smith, J. W. Faull (referee). *Seated:* P. Cranmer, R. J. Longland, D. A. Kendrew, B. C. Gadney (captain), C. Webb, W. H. Weston.
Above 1937 England 6, Scotland 3. H. S. Sever scores England's second try to ensure their first win at Murrayfield and a Triple Crown. Sever had already dropped the goal in England's 4–3 win over Wales and scored the winning try in their 9–8 victory over Ireland.

Above The 1947 Joint Champions beat Scotland 24–5 in the first official international at Twickenham for 8 years. English players (left to right): N. M. Hall, D. F. White, R. H. G. Weighill, J. O. Newton-Thompson (with ball), M. R. Steele-Bodger, J. Heaton (in distance), A. P. Henderson, J. Mycock.
Right (*top*) The 1953 international champions prior to defeating Scotland 26–8. *Standing* (left to right): M. J. Dowling (referee), R. C. Bazley, A. O. Lewis, W. P. C. Davies, J. E. Woodward, S. J. Adkins, W. A. Holmes, J. Butterfield, G. Warden (touch judge). *Seated:* E. Evans, D. T. Wilkins, N. M. Hall (captain), J. Mac G. Kendall-Carpenter, D. F. White, R. V. Stirling. *In front:* D. W. Shuttleworth, M. Regan.
Right (*bottom*) The 1957 Grand Slam XV in action against France at Twickenham. English players (left to right): E. Evans, C. R. Jacobs, P. H. Thompson (5), R. W. D. Marques, J. D. Currie, A. Ashcroft, R. Higgins, R. E. G. Jeeps, P. G. D. Robbins, R. M. Bartlett, J. Butterfield.

Top Evans's men—the Grand Slam team of 1957. *Standing* (left to right): R. C. Williams (referee), J. Butterfield, W. P. C. Davies, P. H. Thompson, R. W. D. Marques, J. D. Currie, P. G. D. Robbins, C. R. Jacobs, R. Challis, N. M. Parkes (touch judge). *Seated:* P. B. Jackson, G. W. Hastings, E. Evans (captain), A. Ashcroft, R. Higgins. *In front:* R. M. Bartlett, R. E. G. Jeeps.
Right 1958 England's first win over Australia. P. B. Jackson on one of his inimitable runs, watched by J. G. G. Hetherington.
Above The 1963 international champions prior to defeating Wales 13–6 at Cardiff. *Standing* (left to right): R. A. Crowe (touch judge), D. C. Manley, S. J. S. Clarke, A. M. Davis, B. J. Wightman, J. E. Owen, B. A. Dovey, N. J. Drake-Lee, J. G. Willcox. *Seated:* D. P. Rogers, M. S. Phillips, J. Roberts, R. A. W. Sharp (captain), P. B. Jackson, J. D. Thorne, M. P. Weston.

Top 1969 England 22, France 8. D. P. Rogers (with headband), making a record 32nd appearance for England, watches R. E. Webb drive through supported by D. L. Powell, K. E. Fairbrother, D. M. Rollitt, P. J. Larter and N. E. Horton. J. F. Finlan is on the right.
Above The first England XV to beat South Africa—1969. *Standing* (left to right): K. D. Kelleher (referee), R. F. Johnson (touch judge), D. J. Duckham, P. M. Hale, B. R. West, P. J. Larter, K. E. Fairbrother, A. L. Bucknall, C. B. Stevens, I. R. Shackleton, N. C. Starmer-Smith, M. H. Titcomb (touch judge). *Seated:* J. S. Spencer, J. V. Pullin, R. Hiller (captain), A. M. Davis, K. J. Fielding, R. B. Taylor.
Right 1969 J. V. Pullin scores the winning try in England's 11–8 victory over South Africa. R. B. Taylor and C. B. Stevens are close at hand.

Top D. J. Duckham, England's most capped back, playing against New Zealand in 1973.
Above England 16, New Zealand 10 at Auckland 1973. F. E. Cotton, A. G. Ripley and J. A. Watkins watch J. G. Webster clear.

B. W. Redwood (Bristol), one of the first spin passers, a useful box kicker and good at linking with his back row, was tried at scrum half and D. H. Prout, a strong running wing, made the fifth Northampton player in the side.

However, the most significant choice was that of R. Hiller (Harlequins) who had made his name scoring 11 of Surrey's 14 points against Durham in the first 1967 county final when these counties shared the championship after a replay. His attacking ability was evident in the way he joined in moves if called, and he made up for a lack of speed by his flair for reading opposition moves, intercepting and coming away. But it is as a kicker of the ball—place, drop and punt—that Hiller will always be remembered.

The new look side shaped well against Wales at Twickenham. Larter, West and Gay shone in the lines, Pullin outhooked Gale and England went ahead with a try by McFadyean. Edwards, partnered with John against England for the first time, equalized round the blind side but Redwood, his opposite number, kicked high and scored himself. Hiller converted this try and when he kicked a penalty England were leading 11–3 in the second half. A knock on led to a scrum from which Wales scored a try converted by Jarratt and John drew the match 11–11 with a dropped goal.

The Irish match, at home, was also drawn. Ireland were 6–3 up when, after thirty minutes, England lost Redwood, concussed, and Bell went scrum half. Nevertheless the depleted side held on. Hiller equalized with a penalty and, after Kiernan had put Ireland 9–6 ahead with his third penalty, made the score 9–9 with a last-minute penalty after Ireland had thrown the ball into touch.

Before 1959 the 'foot after a tackle' law had meant that forwards dribbled on or heeled back, but by 1968 a generation of forwards had emerged whose aim was to pick up the ball. Rucks and mauls became all-important and so much a part of pack drill that it was noted in the Irish match that the English forwards were ruck happy, preferring to charge into a congested area instead of using the open, a rather unfortunate product of disciplined rugby.

However, the pack was not changed again. The backs were held responsible for the poor display against Ireland, and for the last two games T. J. Brooke (Richmond) was brought in to play in the centre alongside his Surrey colleague Lloyd, and M. P. Weston (Durham City) and Pickering were the halves.

Weston was made captain and took his appearances to twenty-nine—the record for an England back until overtaken by Duckham in 1974. He gave England the lead in Paris with a left-footed dropped goal and Hiller's second penalty put England 9–3 ahead in the second half. However, the genius of the Camberabero brothers triumphed in the end. France won 14–9 and went on to their first Grand Slam.

England finished third in the table by winning 8–6 at Murrayfield. Scotland led by a penalty and drop at half-time but an England ploy came off when Coulman, waiting ten yards out, ran on to a long throw over a four-man line-out and crashed through the Scottish defence. Hiller converted and won the match with a penalty.

Both Coulman and Hiller were rewarded with places in the 1968 Lions team to South Africa where one test was drawn and three lost. Hiller scored 104 points in 8 games, his 23 against Border being the highest by a Lion in South Africa until Old's 37 against South Western Districts in 1974. As Kiernan was captain, Hiller did not appear in a Test, but Savage and Taylor played in all four. England's other representatives on the tour were A. L. Horton, Larter, Pullin and West.

Lloyd, who had looked so promising in his first season for England, withdrew after selection and was not seen at international level again because in 1969 England discovered a pair of new centres who looked to be the answer to selectors' dreams.

They were J. S. Spencer (Cambridge) and D. J. Duckham, in only his second season with Coventry. The strong Spencer could run at or outside his man, could be set up for the crash ball, and, when tackled, could stand up and make the ball available to his forwards. Duckham was a dashing sidestepper with an eye for a gap and the sheer speed to utilize it. Nineteen-year-old K. J. Fielding, whose explosive acceleration and swerve were seen to best advantage in sevens—he scored eleven tries for Loughborough Colleges on Middlesex Finals Day at Twickenham in 1970—was on the right wing, and Webb, whose career was plagued by injuries, on the left.

T. C. Wintle (Northampton) was given a full season at

scrum half. His strong wrists and willingness to use the dive pass resulted in a long, fast service that gave his stand-off, Finlan, room to move.

Coulman had signed for Salford and was replaced at loose head by D. L. Powell (Northampton). Pullin, of course, was now a fixture as hooker, and K. E. Fairbrother, a powerful scrummager from Coventry, useful on the peel, was at tight head. Lock with Larter was twenty-year-old N. E. Horton (Moseley). The back row, all of whom had last played in 1967, was Rogers, Rollitt and Greenwood.

J. R. H. Greenwood (Waterloo), a hard-tackling blind side, skilled in back row moves, an excellent reader of the game and an inspiring captain—he led Lancashire to the championship in 1969—was made skipper. England rugby owes him a lot because he persuaded the national team to meet, unofficially and at their own expense, for practice.

Fixtures this season were rotated and England started with Ireland in Dublin where they held the lead four times but lost 15–17. The half-time score was 9–9—three penalties by Hiller to two by Kiernan and an Irish try. Then came one of the most daring English tries of recent years. Finlan broke out of defence in his own 25, Webb received near half-way and Duckham looped him to score in the corner. Ireland took the lead for the first time (14–12) with Kiernan's conversion of Murphy's try. After McGann had dropped a goal, Hiller landed his fourth penalty.

Greenwood was injured the day before the French match at Twickenham, and replaced as flanker by Taylor and as captain by Rogers.

Originally a quick, destructive open side in the traditional light English mould, Rogers had adjusted his play to suit the new laws by playing closer to the scrum, but his wonderful fitness still enabled him to be in two places at once when required, and in 1969 he beat Wakefield's forty-two-year-old record by taking his number of England caps to thirty-four.

This season the 'no direct kicking for touch outside one's own 25' law was introduced, and the first international at Twickenham under the dispensation was spectacular. England won 22–8, their biggest victory over France since 1914.

The pack gave a fine display and were retained for the season. Pullin won the heads 8–3, Larter, Horton and Taylor were conspicious in the lines-out and Rogers and Rollitt stopped the French peels.

Hiller kicked two conversions and three penalties but the game was memorable for the wing play. Fielding swerved past his man and made a try for Rollitt and, when the French were 11–5 down and attacking, turned the game England's way with an eighty-yard try after a kick over the full back's head and dribble at speed. England's last try was by Webb who, typically, came in from the left onto the tackler's weak shoulder and ran through diagonally.

The same side played against Scotland, but, when Fielding was injured after half an hour, T. J. Dalton (Coventry) became England's first replacement. England won 8–3, both tries being scored by Duckham, the first after he had collected a high kick ahead by Finlan and the second after he appeared outside Dalton on the wing.

Victory in the last match at Cardiff would have enabled England to share the championship with Ireland. However Wales won 30–9, M. Richards scoring four tries, and took the title, England again finishing third.

England's 9 points were three penalties by Hiller who thus scored 36 out of his country's 54 points in 1969.

Chapter Nineteen

Who Beat the Springboks? 1969–72

On 20 December 1969, England, at the sixth attempt, achieved the result that had eluded them for over sixty years—victory over South Africa.

Never before had the national side had such a build-up for one match.

Hitherto the 'coach' had been the captain, with varying degrees of advice from the chairman of selectors. At last England followed New Zealand practice and appointed an official coach—D. F. White, the former Northampton wing forward. A thirty-man squad was selected and started monthly training week-ends in August. Further A. E. Agar and his fellow selectors chose the captain—full back Hiller—early, before the trials.

The final side contained five new caps. Three of the previous season's three-quarters—Spencer and Duckham in the centre and Fielding on the wing—were retained. Webb was out of action and the left-wing berth was given to P. M. Hale, whose direct running had brought him 44 tries for Moseley in 1967–8.

There were new halves—I. R. Shackleton and N. C. Starmer-Smith. Shackleton was primarily a defensive stand-off who had a good left boot, came up to tackle his opposite number and covered well. Starmer-Smith, a running scrum half, was a good line kicker and had a long, if slow, service and an excellent reverse pass. He had been a member of the 1966 Oxford team captained by T. P. Bedford (vice-captain of the 1969 Springboks), and was well versed in the South African style of linking up with his forwards.

A. L. Bucknall, the blind-side flanker, had been another protégé of Bedford at Oxford and also knew South African tactics well. The other back row men, Taylor and West, the hooker, Pullin, and one of the locks, Larter, had all played in South Africa for the 1968 Lions and Pullin, Taylor and the tight head, Fairbrother, had toured there with the Barbarians in 1969, so all knew what to expect up front. The pack leadership was given to lock A. M. Davis, hero of Christchurch in 1963, who this season was captaining Staffordshire to its first championship after only six years as an independent county and the remaining place—loose head—went to C. B. Stevens, a new cap but twenty-eight-year-old veteran of many battles for Cornwall. In addition to doing all expected of him in the tight, Stevens handled and ran well—few props have been capable of putting their wing over after a back movement as he did against France in 1973 and running in a try as he did against New Zealand later that year. The England XV was:

R. Hiller (Harlequins, capt.); K. J. Fielding (Loughborough Colleges), D. J. Duckham (Coventry), J. S. Spencer (Cambridge), P. M. Hale (Moseley); I. R. Shackleton (Cambridge), N. C. Starmer-Smith (Harlequins); C. B. Stevens (Penzance and Newlyn), J. V. Pullin (Bristol), K. E. Fairbrother (Coventry), A. M. Davis (Harlequins), P. J. Larter (Northampton), A. L. Bucknall (Richmond), R. B. Taylor, B. R. West (both Northampton).

For the last seven minutes C. S. Wardlow (Carlisle) replaced Hiller, but he only touched the ball once, when it had gone dead!

South Africa: H. O. de Villiers; S. H. Nomis, O. A. Roux, E. Olivier, A. E. van der Watt; P. J. Visagie, D. J. de Villiers (capt.); J. L. Myburgh, D. C. Walton, J. F. K. Marais, I. J. de Klerk, A. E. de Wet, P. J. F. Greyling, T. P. Bedford, A. J. Bates.
M. J. Lawless replaced Olivier in the second half.

England began badly, losing the first six lines-out, and Visagie kicked a penalty after seven minutes. South Africa extended their lead to 8 points after thirty-five minutes when Visagie converted a corner try by Greyling. However, the England pack settled down to play as a unit. Shrewd throwing enabled Larter and West to win the lines; Fairbrother won a terrific duel with the massive Myburgh in the tight, where the

England shove began to deprive the Springboks of clean possession; and Bucknall harried Dawie de Villiers unceasingly.

Before half-time Starmer-Smith took an inside pass from Shackleton and found Bucknall, Fairbrother and Larter inside him. All handled before Larter crashed over.

After an hour's play, South Africa were penalized at a line-out and Hiller made the score 6–8 with a penalty. An interception by Hiller then put England on the attack and Hale was forced into touch near the South African line after a charge down the wing.

Play was halted while an interrupter was removed—this was the 'demo' tour—and a maul formed from the line-out. The ball squirted out and Pullin capped a wonderful all-round performance by pouncing on it for the winning try. Hiller's conversion made the final score 11–8—and leaves Wales as the only country yet to beat the Springboks!

The rest of the 1969–70 season was anti-climax after this Homeric triumph over a side containing some of South Africa's all-time 'greats'—Marais, D. J. de Villiers, Bedford, Visagie, Greyling and Nomis were amongst the country's twelve most capped players, and participated in the slaughter of the 1968 Lions and the 1970 All Blacks.

The Irish match at Twickenham was more notable for the resurrection of their winger Tony O'Reilly, after seven years' absence, than for the Rugby. England were a penalty goal down, when, midway through the second half, Hiller dropped two goals in quick succession from about the same spot forty-five yards out. Shackleton made the game safe at 9–3 with a try.

The Welsh match, also at Twickenham, was thrown away. Taylor appeared in the line to make an overlap and Duckham scored, Hiller converting. Wales replied with a try but M. J. Novak (Harlequins), a big, quick wing with a swerve, scored a try on debut. Hiller converted and his penalty gave England a 13–3 lead at the interval, at which point the French referee retired injured and was replaced by the English touch judge, R. F. Johnson. Tries by John and Williams took the score to 13–9. Time was running out when England had a line-out on its own line. A poor throw-in went over the England jumpers to the tallest Welshman at the back and he put Hopkins over. Williams's conversion gave Wales the lead, 14–13, and John dropped a late goal to make the final score 17–13.

At Murrayfield Scotland won 14–5, Spencer showing unsuspected pace in scoring a magnificent try from half-way.

England made five changes for the last match—France in Paris—but they did not have the desired effect. France led 19–0 and, though tries by Taylor (the new captain) and Spencer, both converted by the new full-back A. M. Jorden (Cambridge and Blackheath) who also kicked a penalty, made the score 19–13, France added 16 points without further reply.

This result meant that France shared the 1970 Championship with Wales, and England shared the wooden spoon with Scotland.

England finished joint third in 1971, but this was perhaps the most disappointing season of modern times as it was the R.F.U.'s Centenary Year.

Part of the celebrations involved a tour by the Fijians in October and November 1970. Their form was erratic. When opponents and conditions allowed them to, they played spectacular Rugby—as witness their 29–9 drubbing of the Barbarians at Gosforth—but, on the other hand, they lost 8–10 to Southern Counties at Bournemouth. The big match of their tour was against England Under-25 at Twickenham and, though England won 15–11, they scored only one try to the two scored by the Fijians in pouring rain that made the visitors' style of play largely ineffective.

Nevertheless, the England selectors attached importance to this result and no fewer than six of the seven new caps they sent to Cardiff were products of the Under-25 match. They were P. A. Rossborough (Coventry), a running full back; J. P. A. G. Janion, a hefty wing from Bedford; I. D. Wright (Northampton), a fly half who was quick off the mark and a useful kicker; J. J. Page (Bedford), a scrum half with a spin pass and an accurate kick; B. F. Ninnes, a Coventry lock; and A. Neary, an open side from Broughton Park, who the previous season had supplied England with two other forwards in B. Jackson and M. Leadbetter.

The promising centre partnership of Duckham and Spencer was split. Duckham was moved to the wing, and into the centre came the well built but nimble C. S. Wardlow (Northampton), who could stay on his feet and distribute the ball when tackled and whose crash tackling in midfield would, it was hoped, prevent a repetition of the 1970 débâcle in Paris.

In the event Wales, under Dawes, won 22–6. Gerald Davies (2) and Bevan scored tries, Taylor converting two. John dropped two goals and Williams landed a penalty. England mustered a try by R. C. Hannaford, the Bristol number 8, making his debut, and a penalty by Rossborough. Wales went on to their first Grand Slam since 1952.

Experience in the form of Hiller, who this season captained Surrey to its first outright county championship, and the Moseley lock N. E. Horton was called on for the visit to Dublin. England won 9–6, thanks to three penalties by Hiller.

Against France at Twickenham England were outplayed in the second half but hung on for a 14–14 draw. Hiller again scored all England's points—three penalties and the conversion of a try scored by himself after P. B. Glover (Bath), a late substitute on the wing, had kicked over the French line. Hiller, in his fourteenth international, thus became the first man to top 100 points for England.

A dramatic last-minute conversion by their skipper P. C. Brown enabled Scotland to win 16–15—their first victory at Twickenham since Shaw's match in 1938. Two more penalties and a try by Hiller meant that he scored 32 points in succession for England before Neary broke his monopoly with a try.

This was the last encounter in the 1971 championship, but England had two matches left. A week after the Calcutta Cup game, England met Scotland again in a fixture at Murrayfield arranged exactly 100 years after the first international of all. This time Scotland won 26–6.

The season ended with a match against Sir William Ramsey's Overseas XV at Twickenham. The brightest galaxy of talent ever assembled undertook a short tour of England in April 1971. At Leicester, they beat Midland, London and Home Counties 18–13; at Birkenhead, the North of England 26–12; and at Bristol, South and South-Western Counties 28–13.

The teams for this, England's sixth international of 1971, were:

England: R. Hiller (Harlequins); J. P. A. G. Janion (Bedford), J. S. Spencer (Headingley, capt.), D. J. Duckham (Coventry), P. B. Glover (Bath); A. R. Cowman (Loughborough Colleges), N. C. Starmer-Smith; C. B. Stevens (both Harlequins), J. V. Pullin (Bristol), F. E. Cotton (Loughborough Colleges),

P. J. Larter (Northampton), C. W. Ralston (Richmond), R. N. Creed (Coventry), P. J. Dixon (Harlequins), A. Neary (Broughton Park).

President's Overseas XV: P. Villepreux (France); B. G. Williams (New Zealand), J. Jansen (South Africa), J. Maso (France), S. Knight (Australia); W. D. Cottrell (New Zealand), D. J. de Villiers; J. F. K. Marais (both South Africa), R. B. Prosser, P. Johnson (both Australia), C. E. Meads (New Zealand), F. C. du Preez (South Africa), I. Kirkpatrick, B. J. Lochore (capt.), (both New Zealand), G. V. Davis (Australia).

At half-time the scores were level—a try by Marais to a penalty by Hiller. After the interval Villepreux converted tries by Kirkpatrick and Williams but, with ten minutes of normal time left, England were only 11–13 behind, Hiller having converted a try by himself and landed another penalty. However, the Overseas XV ran away with the game 28–11, Villepreux converting two more tries by Williams and one by Kirkpatrick.

By yet again scoring all England's points, Hiller took his season's total to 49—three more than Hosen's record in 1967. No full back had scored a try for England since T. W. Fry in 1880 but in 1971 Hiller scored three in one season! He maintained his phenomenal form with the 1971 Lions in New Zealand, where he scored 102 points in his ten matches, though once again he was second-string full-back—this time to J. P. R. Williams.

England's other representatives were Pullin, Duckham, Stevens, Spencer and P. J. Dixon, a rugged back row 'grafter' skilled in winning the ball and in keeping possession, who was selected for the Lions before England. Wardlow cried off the tour with a broken jaw. Pullin hooked in all four Tests. Dixon played in three and scored Britain's only try in the crucial last Test when the 14–14 draw enabled the Lions to finish with two Test wins, one defeat, one draw, and so become the first British side to win a series in New Zealand. Duckham played in the last three Tests where he distinguished himself by his defensive covering. Only in the provincial games—all twenty of which were won—did the Lions throw the ball about and Duckham scored a record six tries against West Coast–Buller.

England's Lions were not included in the tour of Japan, Hong Kong, Singapore and Ceylon undertaken, under the captaincy of D. P. Rogers, to conclude the R.F.U.'s centenary celebrations.

All seven games were won and the points tally was 228 for, 52 against, but the trip was of little use for team-building as in 1972 England, for the first time, lost all four matches in the Five Nations Championship. However, the championship was not completed because Wales and Scotland refused to play in Dublin.

At Twickenham Wales scored the only try of the match and won 12–3. England led Ireland 9–3 at half-time, Hiller having kicked a penalty and converted England's first four-point try—by Ralston—and were 12–10 up in injury time when Flynn scored the winning try and Kiernan's conversion made the final score 16–12.

Hiller was dropped, and retired from international rugby, after the Irish match. In his nineteen matches he had scored 138 points for England. The magnitude of this performance is brought out by two facts. His total was more than double the previous career record for England (63 by Hosen) and, while he was playing, his colleagues mustered only 61 points amongst them.

Dixon was given the captaincy and P. M. Knight of Bristol was made full back. Most of Knight's rugby was played on the wing—in 1971–2 he was the leading try scorer in England—but he was full back for Gloucestershire who this season won their first championship for thirty-five years. His selection meant that he joined three county colleagues in the national side for, as well as the inevitable Pullin, M. A. Burton and A. Brinn were in the pack. These two, incidentally, were from Gloucester, who in 1972 won the first R.F.U. National Club Knock Out when they beat Moseley 17–6 in the final at Twickenham.

Knight's first match was against France in Paris where England lost 37–12. This was the most points ever scored against England, and the only encouraging feature from the visitors' view was the place kicking of their fly half—A. G. B. Old (Middlesbrough). Old kicked two penalties and converted a try by M. C. Beese (Liverpool) who hacked on a kick ahead by Duckham and scored the first try by a three-quarter for England for two years!

Old landed three penalties at Murrayfield, but kicked to the blind-side wing or in front of his forwards and did not pass to his centres until ten minutes after half-time.

Scotland won 23–9 and the England captain was quoted as saying, 'England meant to run the ball but somehow it never happened.'

The omens could hardly have been less propitious for embarking on one of the toughest assignments in world rugger—a short tour of South Africa—particularly as two of England's Test Lions, Duckham and Dixon, were not available. However, some promising newcomers had been blooded in 1972 and they were to carry England through one of the most remarkable periods in the long history of the national side.

Chapter Twenty

A Unique Treble 1972–4

Between June 1972 and November 1973, England accomplished the remarkable feat of beating South Africa, New Zealand and Australia and, for good measure, winning the first world international seven-a-side tournament.

The story started in May 1972, when England, who had hit rock bottom by losing seven internationals in a row, became the last of the Home Countries to undertake a tour of South Africa, where the Lions had not won a Test since 1955 and where Scotland had lost 18–10 at Port Elizabeth in 1960, Ireland 24–8 at Cape Town in 1961 and Wales 24–3 at Durban in 1964. South Africa, unbeaten in their last seven Tests (against New Zealand, France and Australia), claimed to be world champions and England were the first Home Country to be made to play a Test at altitude—Ellis Park, Johannesburg, is 5,700 feet above sea level, 1,300 feet higher than Ben Nevis!

John Elders, the England coach, was given a new captain—John Pullin. Respected as the world's most experienced hooker, Pullin had scored the winning try for England *v.* South Africa at Twickenham in 1969 and had played in all the Tests when the Lions won the series in New Zealand in 1971, so had the confidence that could only come from a man who had played for sides that had beaten the Southern Hemisphere giants. Through touring South Africa twice (with the Lions and the Barbarians), he knew the style of play in the country intimately, and he soon proved that he could instil enthusiasm and motivation into the players under his command.

At least seven likely candidates for the tour were not available and the selectors, aiming at a blend of established and potential England players, included eight uncapped men in the final party of twenty-five.

Before the tour the manager, A. O. Lewis, stated that the first objective was for England to win all seven matches. In fact they won six, drew one and scored 166 points against 58.

Natal (19–0) and Western Province (9–6) were beaten before England made racial history by playing the S.A. Rugby Federation (Coloured) and the S.A. Rugby Board (African) teams. The Northern Transvaal match was drawn 13–13, but Griqualand West were beaten 60–21, the highest score by a British touring team in South Africa (the previous record was 45 by the 1910 Lions against Transvaal Country) and Old's 24 points (the conversion of all nine tries, a penalty and a drop) bettered the previous highest by a British tourist—Hiller's 23 for the 1968 Lions.

The team for the Test included four new caps. One of them was S. A. Doble, a full back whose prodigious place kicking helped bring him 486 points for Moseley in 1971–2, when he totalled 581 in all first-class matches. In a career lasting from 1964 to 1976 Doble scored 3,033 points in 332 games for Moseley, and 303 in 39 championship fixtures for Staffordshire.

Both wings were from Bristol—P. M. Knight, quick and alert for the half-chance, who had scored two tries against Natal and the winning try against Western Province, and A. Morley, whose upright running made him hard to tackle.

Janion was played in the centre, where his crash tackling was decisive, and his partner was P. S. Preece, son of a former England captain. Preece had come to the fore through the area trials instituted in 1971. Though only eleven stone, he relished tackling and had all the attributes—speed, acceleration, side-step, swerve and judgment—of a top class centre.

Old, a good kicker with either foot and a sound tackler, has had few opportunities to show his flair at international level, but was the ideal fly-half for the way England played their Rugby at this time.

J. G. Webster, dropped for L. E. Weston (West of Scotland) in 1972, regained the scrum-half berth. Webster's greatest asset was his immense work-rate which, allied to a fine positional sense, enabled him to be up in attack to make something out of nothing or back in defence to retrieve. His quick service meant that his stand-off was rarely under pressure, his box kicking was first class and, though only 5 ft 5 in., he would take on anybody.

Pullin was propped by C. B. Stevens, a strong man whose wrenching of the ball from the mauls was a feature of the tour, and M. A. Burton, a tight head who loved taking on the opposition.

P. J. Larter, recalled after a season's absence, showed again that Springboks brought the best out of him and proved much harder than his critics claimed. His fellow lock was C. W. Ralston, quick for his size (6 ft 6 in. and 16 st. 7 lb.), a good ball player and increasingly dominant in the lines-out.

A. Neary, A. G. Ripley and J. A. Watkins formed one of the best back rows in England's history.

Neary, deceptively fast to the break-down and aggressive with the ball in his hands, had developed a line from open side that enabled him to arrive at the fly-half with the ball in the old style. Ripley was making great strides at number 8 for one who played soccer until he was eighteen; his 6 ft 5 in. was invaluable at the back of the lines and he was particularly dangerous going forward. Watkins, the blind side, a late inclusion in the party, was a players' player whose tackling, retrieving and setting up made him the discovery of the tour.

England's team was:

S. A. Doble (Moseley); A. J. Morley (Bristol), J. P. A. G. Janion (Bedford), P. S. Preece (Coventry), P. M. Knight (Bristol); A. G. B. Old (Middlesbrough), J. G. Webster (Moseley); C. B. Stevens (Penzance and Newlyn), J. V. Pullin (Bristol, capt.), M. A. Burton (Gloucester), C. W. Ralston (Richmond), P. J. Larter (Northampton), J. A. Watkins (Gloucester), A. G. Ripley (Rosslyn Park), A. Neary (Broughton Park).

South Africa: R. A. Carlson; S. H. Nomis, O. A. Roux, J. S. Jansen, G. H. Muller; D. S. Snyman, J. F. Viljoen; J. T. Sauermann, J. F. B. van Wyk, N. S. Bezuidenhout, J. G. Williams, P. G. du Plessis, J. H. Ellis, A. J. Bates, P. J. F. Greyling (capt.).

The result—England 18, South Africa 9—was the biggest upset in rugby history and meant that England were the first touring team from any country to leave South Africa unbeaten since the first British 'missionary' tour of 1891.

England's was a team effort with everyone playing for each other.

The law change which allowed the fumble meant that there were fewer knock-ons and therefore fewer scrums and fewer opportunities for the Springbok heavyweights to grind their opponents down. As it was, the English front row won the heads 2–1. Larter, Ralston and Ripley took their share of line-out ball and, most significantly, the English forwards were quicker to the loose ball and made more intelligent use of it. Janion and Preece tackled the South African centres out of the game and the whole side were prepared to cover.

Snyman kicked an early penalty. Doble replied. Snyman kicked another. Doble again equalized, and, with the last kick of the first half, put England 9–6 ahead with his third penalty.

England's halves were keeping the ball in front of their forwards and two minutes after the interval Webster hoisted a high kick that made the South African full-back stretch and fumble. Webster was on the ball in a flash and whipped it out to Morley who broke a tackle in speeding twenty yards for the only try of the match. Doble converted from touch and had kicked his fourth penalty before Snyman put his third over. England's courage in the closing stages was epitomized by Stevens, who left the field and returned with six stitches in his head.

The last words on this famous victory come from the 1973 South African Rugby Annual: 'England's real heroes were Doble and little Webster. Doble, never found wanting for a moment on defence, booted four penalties and a conversion for a tally of 14 points. Webster deserves a medal, not only because his kick opened the way to Morley's try but because he took on and beat the world's best flanks. His sniping breaks and clever little kicks were always a menace.'

Hopes were naturally high for the 1972–3 season at home which opened with the visit of the Seventh All Blacks. Not only had England achieved the impossible in South Africa, but New Zealand had been defeated on English soil for the only time except when England beat them in 1936 (Obolensky's match).

At Workington the following North-Western Counties side won 16–14:

B. J. O'Driscoll (Manchester); A. A. Richards (Fylde), C. S. Wardlow (Coventry), D. Roughley (Liverpool), P. S. Maxwell (Richmond); A. R. Cowman (Coventry), S. J. Smith (Sale); F. E. Cotton (Loughborough Colleges, capt.), J. Lansbury (Sale), W. F. Anderson (Orrell), M. Leadbetter (Broughton Park), R. Trickey (Sale), D. Robinson, P. J. Dixon (both Gosforth), A. Neary (Broughton Park).

A fortnight later the All Blacks lost 16–8 to this Midland Counties (West) team at Moseley:

S. A. Doble (Moseley); D. J. Duckham (Coventry, capt.), M. K. Swain (Moseley), P. S. Preece (Coventry), M. J. Cooper; J. F. Finlan, J. G. Webster (all Moseley); T. F. Corless (Birmingham), J. D. Gray, K. E. Fairbrother (both Coventry), N. E. Horton, L. S. Smith, I. N. Pringle, J. C. White (all Moseley), T. Cowell (Rugby).

For the international at Twickenham, England intended to stick to the South African heroes, apart from the recall of Duckham, who had been unable to tour, and the introduction of the strong but inexperienced P. J. Warfield who was played at inside centre. However, Old withdrew with an injury that was to keep him out of all the season's internationals and was replaced by Finlan, who this year captained North Midlands to its first county semi-final since 1948. Also, injuries to Cotton and Burton led to the capping of Anderson from Orrell, a club that had come to the front in the National Knock-out and supplied four men to the Lancashire side which won the 1973 county championship. Teams:

England: S. A. Doble (Moseley); A. J. Morley (Bristol), P. J. Warfield (Durham University), P. S. Preece, D. J. Duckham (both Coventry); J. F. Finlan, J. G. Webster (both Moseley); C. B. Stevens (Penzance and Newlyn), J. V. Pullin (Bristol, capt.), W. F. Anderson (Orrell), C. W. Ralston (Richmond), P. J. Larter (Northampton), J. A. Watkins (Gloucester), A. G. Ripley (Rosslyn Park), A. Neary (Broughton Park).

New Zealand: J. F. Karam; G. B. Batty, B. J. Robertson, B. G. Williams; R. M. Parkinson, I. N. Stevens; S. M. Going; K. K. Lambert, R. W. Norton, G. J. Whiting, H. H. MacDonald, P. J. Whiting, A. J. Wyllie, A. R. Sutherland, I. A. Kirkpatrick (capt.).

England, content to contain New Zealand up front, had their chances but muffed them. Kirkpatrick scored the only try of the match, Karam converted, Williams dropped a goal and the All Blacks won 9–0.

Three weeks later Duckham, Pullin and an uncapped Cambridge lock, R. M. Wilkinson, had the consolation of participating in the Barbarians' classic 23–11 victory over the All Blacks at Cardiff.

In 1971 Loughborough Colleges had won the first Universities Athletic Union final staged at Twickenham and two of their side, A. R. Cowman, a running fly half, and F. E. Cotton, a prop extraordinarily mobile for his 16½ stone whose good hands and strength enabled him to excel on the peel and in the loose, were capped by England. Both had helped North-Western Counties beat the 1972 All Blacks and they returned to the national side for the match at Cardiff. However, the Arms Park bogy remained, and Wales won 25–9.

There were four changes for the Irish match at Dublin. P. J. Dixon, another hero of North-Western Counties historic victory, and A. M. Jorden, a reliable two-footed full back from Blackheath, were old caps, but there were two debutants.

At scrum half the long spin pass of S. J. Smith (Sale) was preferred to the shorter, but quicker, service of Webster and R. M. Uttley (Gosforth) established himself at lock.

A versatile player with much experience in the back row, Uttley is the type of lock required in the modern game where speed to the rucks and mauls and the strength to tear the ball out and set it up are just as important as the old second-row virtues of shoving and jumping. In fact, though a competent line-out man, Uttley was rarely used now that it had been realized that ball from 2 or 3 is usually negative. Line-out ball from Ralston at number 5 and Ripley at the back was much more useful if England's backs were to avoid the attention of opposing flankers from the end of lines-out.

Ireland had been the only Home Country the All Blacks did not beat—they drew 10–10—and they defeated England 18–9. But at least England turned up—no Home Country had played in Dublin for two years.

For the two remaining matches at Twickenham England reverted to a kicking fly half, M. J. Cooper, the second Moseley man to occupy the position in 1973. His club position was left wing but he was Staffordshire's stand-off.

The formula worked, or perhaps ground advantage was the decisive factor because in 1973, for the only time, all five countries won both their home matches and the championship ended in a quintuple tie.

Against France there was the refreshing sight of wing tries after centre breaks. After Jorden had kicked a penalty, Preece broke through and ran sixty yards before giving Duckham a perfectly timed scoring pass. This was Duckham's first try for England since 1970 when he was still a centre. In the second half, G. W. Evans, a Coventry centre with a double-shuffle swerve and the rare ability to build up pace, stop, side-step and build up pace again, burst through and Stevens was on hand to put Duckham over for his second try. Jorden added a penalty and England won 14–6—their first victory in the championship for two years.

The form was maintained in the Calcutta Cup match when Scotland were beaten 20–13. Cooper missed out his centres to put over P. J. Squires, a wing from Harrogate, and the hard-working Dixon showed his strength and facility for being on the ball by crashing over for two tries. Jorden converted one and England led 14–0 before a Scottish rally produced 13 points. However, Evans went over after Preece had kicked high to the Scottish posts, and Jorden's conversion made the game safe.

But his was not the end of England's international season as, to celebrate their centenary, the Scottish R.U. staged a world seven-a-side competition at Murrayfield.

Coventry were the most successful English club in 1972–3, when they won forty matches, scored 1,153 points and beat Bristol 27–15 in the R.F.U. Club Knock-out Final, and four of their men, Duckham, Preece, Rossborough and hooker J. D. Gray, represented England at the tournament. The other major influence was Loughborough Colleges who provided the captain, Cotton, and ex-students in Fielding, Gray and S. J. Smith, and the Loughborough style of sevens was adopted.

In Group B England beat France 22–0, the President's VII (who included South Africans) 26–16 and, most gratifying of all, Wales—Edwards, Gerald Davies, Taylor, Williams and company—24–10.

In the final England met Mike Gibson's Ireland (who had

won Group A by defeating New Zealand, Australia and Scotland) with the following VII:

K. J. Fielding (Moseley), P. S. Preece, P. A. Rossborough (both Coventry), S. J. Smith (Sale); F. E. Cotton (Loughborough Colleges), J. D. Gray (Coventry), A. G. Ripley (Rosslyn Park). Rossborough replaced Duckham, injured in an earlier game.

England came from behind to win 22–18 when Fielding scored his ninth try of the day, Gray converting, and so won the only international sevens ever held.

All the seven were in England's party selected to tour the Argentine in August 1973. Owing to threats by urban guerillas, this tour was cancelled and Fielding and Gray had turned professional by the time England left for a hastily arranged short tour to New Zealand, who themselves had cancelled a visit by the Springboks.

En route, England beat Fiji 13–12, but they found the New Zealand provinces too much for them and lost to Taranaki, Wellington and Canterbury—all strong unions included in the itinerary to ensure big gates and make a short tour pay.

The English players had had no match practice since April and were taking on men at the height of their season, and used to the new line-out laws, so few gave much for England's chances in their fourth and last match in New Zealand—the Test at Eden Park, Auckland, on 15 September 1973.

The teams were:

New Zealand: R. N. Lendrum; G. B. Batty, I. A. Hurst, B. G. Williams; R. M. Parkinson, J. P. Dougan; S. M. Going; K. K. Lambert, R. W. Norton, M. G. Jones, H. H. MacDonald, S. C. Strahan, K. W. Stewart, A. J. Wyllie, I. A. Kirkpatrick (capt.). T. Morrison replaced Parkinson after fifty-five minutes.

England: P. A. Rossborough; D. J. Duckham, P. S. Preece, G. W. Evans (all Coventry), P. J. Squires (Harrogate); A. G. B. Old (Leicester), J. G. Webster (Moseley); C. B. Stevens (Penzance and Newlyn), J. V. Pullin (Bristol, capt.), F. E. Cotton (Coventry), C. W. Ralston (Richmond), R. M. Uttley (Gosforth), J. A. Watkins (Gloucester), A. G. Ripley (Rosslyn Park), A. Neary (Broughton Park).

Against all the odds, England won 16–10.

Terry McLean, doyen of New Zealand journalists, reported: 'The All Blacks were hammered, outfought forward. And this, I tell you, is no fairy story. New Zealand, moreover, were outthought in general tactics.'

The England shove had the All Blacks going backwards and at times their front row were lifted. Ralston outjumped Strahan. The England back row and scrum half tied up Going, the key to New Zealand's play, whose life was made even more uncomfortable by the way the England fowards poured through the new line-out gaps on to him if the All Blacks did win the ball.

New Zealand took an early lead with a blind-side try by Batty but Webster broke after a move with his back row and, when Preece was tackled, Squires was up for the try. Rossborough, who had an excellent all-round game, put England ahead with his conversion into the wind. M. J. Cooper (Moseley) had no sooner come on as an 'emergency' for the injured Evans than Hurst went over. Lendrum converted and New Zealand led 10–6 at the interval.

England, with the wind at their backs in the second half, continued with their tactics of kicking by their halves, using their three-quarters for chasing and tackling. They needed only seven minutes to regain the lead. Webster was on to a poor clearance by New Zealand's full-back and Ralston sent Stevens running in. Rossborough's conversion put England ahead and late in the game Webster kicked high, was up to gather and feed Old who sent Neary over.

England in the words of manager D. L. Sanders had 'won the one that mattered' and gained their first victory over New Zealand for thirty-seven years. As well as being the only Home Country to beat South Africa home and away, they had also become the only Home Country to beat New Zealand home and away.

A short tour by Australia in the autumn of 1973 gave England the opportunity of defeating all the Southern Hemisphere countries in the space of eighteen months. This they took to the tune of 20–3. Teams:

England: P. A. Rossborough (Coventry); P. J. Squires (Harrogate), J. P. A. G. Janion (Bedford), D. Roughley (Liverpool), D. J. Duckham (Coventry); A. G. B. Old

(Leicester), S. J. Smith (Sale); C. B. Stevens (Penzance and Newlyn), J. V. Pullin (Bristol, capt.), F. E. Cotton (Coventry), C. W. Ralston (Richmond), R. M. Uttley (Gosforth), J. A. Watkins (Gloucester), A. G. Ripley (Rosslyn Park), A. Neary (Broughton Park).

Australia: R. L. Fairfax; L. Monaghan, R. D. L'Estrange, G. A. Shaw, J. J. McLean; P. G. Rowles, J. N. B. Hipwell (capt.); S. G. MacDougall, C. M. Carberry, R. Graham, G. Fay, S. C. Gregory, M. R. Cocks, A. A. Shaw, B. R. Battishall.

Neary, Ripley and Old scored tries. Rossborough converted one and kicked two penalties. Fairfax replied with a penalty for Australia.

Preece was out for the season with cartilage trouble but Evans was fit for all the 1974 home internationals, for which Dixon replaced Watkins at blind side.

At Murrayfield a missed kick for touch in injury time and an offside before the ball had gone dead cost England the Calcutta Cup and, as it happened, a share in the championship.

Scotland led 9–0 before Cotton charged over and Old, with his only place kick of the game, landed a penalty, to make the interval score 9–7. A typical high-stepping surge by Ripley led to a try by Neary, putting England 11–9 ahead. A try from full-back Irvine regained the lead for Scotland at 13–11, only for Rossborough to make it 14–13 to England with a forty-yard dropped goal. Then Irvine punished England's carelessness by landing a penalty from touch with the last kick of the match and snatched a 16–14 victory for the Scots.

At Twickenham there was the unwelcome sight of Ireland leading 26 points to 9 (three penalties by Old). Old, whose immaculate place kicking brought him 17 points in the match, converted a try by Squires and landed two more penalties, but Ireland won 26–21 and, by becoming the only side for two years to win a championship match away from home, went on to become Five Nations Champions for the first time in twenty-three years.

Having lost these two games, England were left with the daunting prospect of playing France in their new Parc des Princes Stadium, where all previous visitors, including the

Seventh All Blacks, had lost, and taking on the unbeaten Welsh XV.

England rose to the occasion magnificently.

A drop and a penalty by Romeu gave France a 6–0 interval lead. Evans dropped a goal but Romeu, with a try and conversion, put France 12–3 ahead. However, Old landed a penalty from near touch and England broke from their own half. K. Smith, a new cap from Roundhay who had shone in the North's 53–12 massacre of the Midlands in an area trial and was making his debut in the centre, and Evans handled before Duckham raced in after a typical inside feint and outside swerve. Old's conversion drew the match 12–12.

For the Welsh match at Twickenham the selectors, daringly, blooded W. H. Hare (Notts) who had come to notice earlier in the season when he scored two tries from full back in England Under-23s' 19–10 win over Japan. The three-quarters were Squires, K. Smith, Evans and Duckham; the halves Old and Webster; the forwards Stevens, Pullin, Burton, Ralston, Uttley, Dixon, Ripley, Neary.

England chose to play against the wind and scored first when Evans scissored with Old and linked up with his locks who enabled Duckham, making his thirtieth appearance for England (a record for a back), to score. Old added a penalty but a try by M. Davies and a conversion and penalty by Bennett gave Wales a 9–7 lead at half-time. Ripley picked up and forced his way over, Old's conversion making the score 13–9. Though Bennett reduced the deficit to one point with a penalty Old replied in kind to make the score at no side England 16, Wales 12.

England had deprived Wales of their unbeaten record and stopped them winning the 1974 international championship.

More important, though, Pullin (for whom 1974 was indeed a memorable year—he overtook Rogers' record of thirty-four appearances for England and led Gloucestershire to their eleventh championship) and his men had erased the one blot on an unparalleled record.

England had not beaten Wales for eleven years. Their victory meant that in the short span of three years—1971 to 1974—England had beaten all the other seven international countries.

Chapter Twenty-One

Anti-climax 1975–6

The memorable wins over South Africa in 1972, New Zealand in 1973 and Wales in 1974 raised hopes that an outstanding side would emerge, but England lost nine of the eleven matches they played in 1975 and 1976.

England had contributed F. E. Cotton, R. M. Uttley, C. W. Ralston, M. A. Burton, A. G. Ripley, A. Neary, A. G. B. Old, G. W. Evans and, as a replacement, A. J. Morley to McBride's Lions, who in 1974 were unbeaten in South Africa with twenty-one wins and one draw—in the last Test, at Johannesburg, where England had triumphed in 1972 but where the British Isles have only won once since 1896.

Cotton and Uttley (as a flanker) played in all four Tests and Cotton was given his country's captaincy in 1975 when England were under new management, John Burgess, very successful with Lancashire, North-Western Counties and North of England sides, taking over as coach.

All those selected for the first international—*v.* Ireland in Dublin—had played for England in 1974 except the centres, P. J. Warfield, who had re-established his claim with thrustful displays for England Under 23's against Tonga (won 40–4) and for Cambridge in the Varsity match, and P. S. Preece, back after missing a season because of injury. Both of these players, together with D. J. Duckham, Cotton and Uttley, had shared in the Barbarians' 13–13 draw at Twickenham with the All Blacks, who had just completed a victorious tour of Ireland to mark that country's centenary.

However, Burton was withdrawn from England's team by the Rugby Football Union as the result of an incident in Gloucestershire's county quarter-final and Uttley cried off to admit a new cap, W. B. Beaumont (Fylde).

England scored from their first real attack, P. J. Squires demonstrating his running swerve, executed without change of pace, to send C. B. Stevens over. Old, recovered from an injury that had ended his Lions tour of South Africa during his fourth match, converted and dropped a goal to put England 9–6 ahead after a try by the ageless Gibson had enabled Ireland to equalize. England looked to be in control until ten minutes from 'No-side' when a careless pass let Gibson take play to the English line and a misunderstanding saw McCombe score a gift try which he converted to give Ireland a 12–9 victory.

For the French match at Twickenham there were four changes. Amongst those axed were John Pullin, after thirty-seven appearances (thirty-six of them consecutive), and Alan Old, perhaps the best place-kicker England has ever had in terms of success ratio. England gave a hesitant, lethargic performance and, although P. A. Rossborough scored 16 of their 20 points (including a try from full-back), France's flair brought them 27 points—the most by any country against England at Twickenham.

There was little improvement at Cardiff. A. M. Jorden (Bedford) captained Eastern Counties to the second county final in their history in 1975 and was recalled again as full-back, but missed all his kicks at goal. England had to send on two replacements—S. J. Smith for J. G. Webster and Pullin for P. J. Wheeler (Leicester)—and, though N. E. Horton, the Moseley captain, caught a Welsh throw-in and crashed over, Wales won easily 20–4.

However, England won the Calcutta Cup match at Twickenham by 7 points to 6.

They made no fewer than eight changes. Cotton withdrew ill and handed over the captaincy to Neary, while Duckham was dropped after thirty-three appearances. Gloucestershire's feat in reaching their sixth successive county final was recognized by the recall of Morley, Burton and D. M. Rollitt, the last-named after six years' absence.

J. J. Page (Northampton and Eastern Counties), out of favour since 1971, was restored to scrum-half and his kicking proved useful, especially when England were under extreme pressure in the closing stages. The home defence was sound and Scotland were confined to two penalty goals. W. N. Bennett, the Bedford fly-half and England's only new cap, landed one and Warfield kicked ahead for Morley to score the winning try.

Thus Scotland were deprived of their first Triple Crown since 1938 and England's 1975 home season ended on a victorious note.

There followed England's first full tour of Australia where they had played once previously—an international at Sydney on the way back from New Zealand in 1963 when torrential rain led to locals dubbing the game 'The Big Wet'.

For their 1975 tour, England's original selection of 25 included twelve uncapped players and only Neary (as captain), Squires, Cotton, Pullin, Uttley and Ripley of the men who had won the Test in New Zealand two years previously. The rest of the party was based on men who had played for successful teams during the winter: England Under-23, Gloucestershire (County Champions for the twelfth time) and Bedford (Club Knock-out winners under the veteran 'Budge' Rogers) supplying most of the tourists.

The tour opened auspiciously with a 64–3 win over Western Australia, fly-half Bennett totalling 36 points (8 conversions, a dropped goal, three penalties and two tries) and winger Morley scoring four tries.

However, matters were different in the east. Sydney won 14–10 and New South Wales Country 14–13, although New South Wales were beaten 29–24, Preece (only in the party because Warfield had withdrawn) obtaining four tries.

Preece was unfit for the first Test by when K. Smith and Cotton were out of the tour injured and scrum-half W. B. Ashton (Orrell) had had to return home.

Two more uncapped players were amongst the three replacements flown out and one of them, B. G. Nelmes, the Cardiff and Gloucestershire loose head, found himself propping against Australia at Sydney. Altogether, England used six new caps in the first Test—Nelmes; full-back P. E. Butler (Gloucester) who in three seasons of first-class Rugby had scored 1,415 points, including 574 in 1973–4; centre A. W. Maxwell (New Brighton); scrum-half P. Kingston (Gloucester); lock N. D. Mantell (Rosslyn Park) and fly-half A. J. Wordsworth (Cambridge University) who came on after fifteen minutes as substitute for Bennett.

Eight minutes later Neary was also put out of the tour by

injury and Pullin took over the captaincy. The England team manager A. O. Lewis was quoted in the Sydney *Sun-Herald* as saying after the match, 'It was a pity those two of ours who went off were such key men. What with one thing and another, we finished the game with about forty per cent of our first-choice team not there.' Small wonder that Australia won 16–9.

By this time it was obvious that the youth policy had failed and, rather than risk tyros, England sent for Old and Dixon.

Within four days of flying in, Old was outside half in the second Test at Brisbane and he scored 13 of England's points, one of his penalties, from a yard inside his own half, being amongst the longest successful place-kicks in England's history.

Squires added a try to the one he scored in the first Test and Uttley went over after the hooter had gone, but Australia's 30–21 victory enabled them to win their first series for ten years.

The game—and the tour—was marred by flying boots and fists and Burton was sent off in the fourth minute for a late tackle.

The Australians' Rugby was much stronger than it had been when they toured England in 1973, although whether getting retaliation in first should be carried to such extremes was queried by former Australian stars John Thornett and Ken Catchpole.

The lessons of the tour as far as England was concerned were that opponents must never be under-estimated and that the strongest available party should always be sent overseas, including reserves who might find themselves pitched into the Test team in case of injuries. Any other view can lead to the devaluation of an England cap.

In an attempt to build up a winning team for the 1975–6 season, England, under a new coach (P. J. Colston of Bristol), reverted to a system of trials that had been discarded fifty years previously on the grounds that full justice could not be done to two candidates for one position from the same region.

For the record, the basic pattern of English trials, with variations due to the visits of touring teams and occasional extra trials such as Champion County *v.* The Rest arranged by zealous (or worried!) selection committees, was:

1874–1909: North *v.* South—sometimes two fixtures a season, with the second before the Calcutta Cup match. (In this series the South won 27, the North 14 and three were drawn.)

1910–24: England *v.* North. England *v.* South. England *v.* The Rest.

1925–70: Whites *v.* Colours. Probables *v.* Possibles. England *v.* The Rest.

1971–1974: Two area trials involving 'South-East and Metropolitan', 'Midlands', 'South-West and South' and 'North', followed by Probables *v.* Possibles and England *v.* The Rest.

1975: England *v.* North and Midlands. England *v.* South and West. England *v.* The Rest.

The 'England' XV that beat 'The Rest' in the last trial of 1975 actually played in the first international of 1976 when decisive revenge for the humiliations suffered 'Down Under' seven months before was obtained at Twickenham. Australia were beaten 23–6. Only nine of the thirty tourists were given a chance to redeem themselves.

For years, Oxbridge, the Hospitals, the Services and the County Championship were fruitful sources for England's teams. For various reasons the first three sources now have much less talent in their ranks. Nor is supreme fitness any longer their prerogative—the growth of training and coaching has enabled clubs to surpass them.

However, although standards of play in the County Championship have deteriorated too, the practice of looking at sides successful in the competition has remained and two of the new caps against Australia—B. J. Corless, a centre, and M. Keyworth, a flanker—came from the North Midlands team that won the Midland group. The third new cap, M. S. Lampkowski, a tank-like scrum-half, came from the England Under-23 XV that beat Italy 29–13 at Gosforth.

In the first match played by a major touring team under floodlights, hooker P. J. Wheeler had led Midland Counties East to an 11–8 victory over the Australians on his home ground (Leicester)—these Wallabies' only defeat in a provincial game apart from Cardiff—and he, Duckham and Cooper, all of whom had been discarded by England in 1975, were recalled.

The teams were:

England: A. J. Hignell (Cambridge University); P. J. Squires (Harrogate), A. W. Maxwell (Headingley), B. J. Corless, D. J. Duckham (both Coventry); M. J. Cooper (Moseley), M. S. Lampkowski (Headingley); F. E. Cotton (Sale), P. J. Wheeler (Leicester), M. A. Burton (Gloucester), W. B. Beaumont (Fylde), R. M. Wilkinson (Bedford), M. Keyworth (Swansea), A. G. Ripley (Rosslyn Park), A. Neary (Broughton Park, capt.).

Australia: P. E. McLean; P. G. Batch, W. A. McKid, G. A. Shaw (capt.), L. E. Monaghan; L. J. Weatherstone, R. G. Hauser; S. C. Finnane, P. A. Horton, S. G. MacDougall, R. A. Smith, D. W. Hillhouse, G. Cornelson, M. E. Loane, A. A. Shaw.

Hignell, who had skippered English Schools from scrum-half in 1974 when they were the only side to defeat the first Australian Schools touring team, had been turned into a full-back by Cambridge. As a nineteen-year-old, he had played for England at Brisbane on the 1975 tour and at the end of the year he scored 19 points in the Varsity match, a record for this 103-year-old fixture. He now kicked the two penalties that gave England a 6–3 lead at half-time.

The England pack ground the Australians down and two of the debutants, Corless and Lampkowski, scored tries. After seventy-five minutes, Duckham received the first of his two passes to cross for a try. Hignell converted and, with the last kick of the game, added his third penalty to make England's total 23—their highest in eighty-seven years of matches against touring teams and their highest in any international for nine years.

The euphoria was short lived. A fortnight later Wales registered their biggest victory at Twickenham, 21–9, in a match notable for two tries from full back by J. P. R. Williams and one try by Gareth Edwards, who this season set new Welsh records with eighteen tries and forty-five appearances.

England, who suffered an unprecedented series of injuries in 1976—Uttley, Corless, Morley, Cooper (twice), Hignell and Wheeler all had to be withdrawn from teams after selection—lost Squires, their most dangerous back, in the first half with a broken arm. Wales, fired by their spirit of nationalism and selected by their 'Big Five' (three of whom were still in their thirties and had played modern international Rugby) from seven first-class clubs playing the same brand of Rugby, went on to equal England's record of seven Grand Slams.

At Murrayfield England finished with two replacements in the three-quarter line, Duckham and Maxwell going off. Despite a spectacular try from the home 22-metres line in which even prop A. B. Carmichael, the new Scottish record cap-holder, handled, England were not behind until after an hour's play but Scotland forged ahead to win 22–12.

Against a poor Irish side at Twickenham, England gave a wretched display. With the wind, they led 9–0 at half-time but the visitors won by 13 points to 12 (four penalty goals by Old, who had had his third recall to the England side the previous match).

Given a week to find players for the trip to Paris, the selectors turned to sides still in the John Player Cup (hitherto the R.F.U. Club Knock-Out Competition) and took S. J. Smith from Sale and P. J. Dixon from Gosforth. Hignell, Cooper and Wheeler were not fully fit when selected and their places were taken by Butler, fly-half C. G. Williams and Pullin, all members of the Gloucestershire team that in 1976 won the county title for a record thirteenth time. During the season Butler scored 90 of Gloucestershire's 126 points, including all 24 against Middlesex in the final.

K. C. Plummer (Bristol), recalled after seven years, D. A. Cooke (Harlequins) and M. A. C. Slemen (Liverpool) had all been brought into the three-quarters in earlier matches so that no back lasted the whole season, Maxwell having been replaced at Murrayfield. This meant that in two years 46 men played for England in internationals, with five more going to Australia and remaining uncapped.

France, looking in a different class, won by 30 points to 9 and England for the second time had lost all four matches in the Five Nations Championship.

England's rugby had reached a very low ebb.

Chapter Twenty-Two

Breaking Even 1977–8

The sorry plight of England's rugby caused the 1976–7 President of the Rugby Football Union, Dick Jeeps, at forty-four one of the youngest men to hold the office in modern times, to involve himself in the future of the national side to an unprecedented degree.

D. L. ('Sandy') Sanders, who believed in discipline both on and off the field, was recalled as chairman of the selectors. England had conceded 86 points (including 13 tries) in their four championship matches in 1976 and Sanders said, 'I see nothing negative in choosing a side that we hope will make it more difficult for our opponents to score.' Emphasis was placed on a strong man as captain and the choice fell on Roger Uttley from Gosforth, who had won the first R.F.U. Club Competition for the John Player Cup in 1976 and won it again in 1977.

Gosforth were also one of the two clubs with 100 per cent records in the official R.F.U. Club Merit Tables introduced in 1976–7. They won all their 'merit' matches in the North, as did Moseley in the Midlands. Although the best of county rugby was recognized by the selection of four men from the 1977 County Champions Lancashire, who in their semi-final had ended Gloucestershire's hopes of appearing in eight successive county finals, England's 1977 XV showed a distinct bias towards club rugby. Indeed, two of the national side had opted out of county football altogether.

Uttley was played for England in his club position of number eight, and the selection of thirty-one-year-old M. Young, winning his first cap at scrum-half seven years after his season as England's travelling reserve, and of P. J. Dixon on the flank ensured Gosforth team work round the base of the scrum. P. J. Wheeler, the hooker, was given his Leicester loose head,

R. J. Cowling, another veteran, and care was taken that the pack played in their exact club positions. This meant that Fran Cotton was tight head and Nigel Horton, the Moseley captain, played international rugby for the first time at left lock.

In both 1975 and 1976 twenty-eight men had appeared for England in the international championship but in 1977 the same team was selected for all four games. It was:

A. J. Hignell (Cambridge University); P. J. Squires (Harrogate), B. J. Corless (Moseley), C. P. Kent (Rosslyn Park), M. A. C. Slemen (Liverpool); M. J. Cooper (Moseley), M. Young (Gosforth); R. J. Cowling, P. J. Wheeler (both Leicester), F. E. Cotton (Sale), N. E. Horton (Moseley), W. B. Beaumont (Fylde), P. J. Dixon, R. M. Uttley, captain (both Gosforth), M. Rafter (Bristol).

Rafter, a hard-tackling, mauling flanker, great-nephew of Sam Tucker, the former England hooker, cried off from the Irish match and was replaced by A. Neary (Broughton Park), and S. J. Smith (Sale) came on at half-time in the French match after Young had broken his nose, but these were the only changes.

For the first time England opened their campaign by receiving Scotland at Twickenham where the Scots have only won thrice in sixty-eight years. England gained an impressive 26–6 victory, the 20-point margin being their biggest in internationals since Ireland were beaten 20–0 twenty-one years before, and their biggest ever over Scotland in the 106-year-old history of the fixture.

A crash-ball scissors enabled Kent, a 14½ stone centre who had showed his power in scoring three tries in England Under-23's 58–15 win over Japan earlier in the season, to set up a ruck from which Cooper sent the left winger Slemen over on the blind side. After Uttley had twice tried to force his way through from scrums near the Scottish line, the Scots expected another attempt but this time the ball was heeled to Young who darted over. Hignell, full back of the Cambridge side that in 1976 had set a Varsity match record by gaining their fifth win in a row over Oxford, added the conversion to a previous penalty and after the interval kicked another penalty.

Another crash-ball to Kent saw the Somerset centre blast through for a solo try, and Uttley picked up and crashed over for a try which Hignell converted to complete the scoring.

Scotland were limited to two penalties and England's defence in 1977 was certainly tighter—they conceded only three tries in their four matches—but they had displayed their tricks—dummy scissors, crash-ball and scrum-half/back row moves—to the watching world and scored only one more try themselves.

That was in the next match—at Lansdowne Road—and was the result of improvisation, Nigel Horton hacking the ball on for Cooper to touch down in the corner. Ireland came back, but 4–0 was the final score and, for the first time since 1960, England had won their first two matches in the Five Nations Championship.

A magnificent effort by the England pack, especially by the 6 foot 5 inch, 16½ stone lock Nigel Horton, whose jumping dominated the line-out on each side's throw-in, deserved to win the French game at Twickenham. England played to force France to concede penalties under pressure. They did, but Hignell kicked only one and that after he had dropped an aimless kick and let France set up a ruck from which they scored a try. France's 4–3 victory was much the closest result in their second Grand Slam season.

At Cardiff, Hignell had a fine game as full-back and gave England a 6–0 lead with two penalties, but Wales led 7–6 at the interval. After Hignell's third penalty had put England 9–7 ahead, Wales replied with a try from full back J. P. R. Williams (his fifth against England) and a penalty. Their 14–9 win meant that England had to be content with third place in the Championship and that Wales equalled England's record of fourteen Triple Crowns.

Half of England's pack—Cotton, Wheeler, Horton and Uttley—were selected to tour New Zealand with the 1977 Lions, together with Neary, a former captain, and Squires, the only back deemed worth a place. However, Uttley withdrew at the last moment with back trouble that has kept him out of the game subsequently and Horton broke a thumb in his fourth game and returned home before going to France and joining Stade Toulousain. Horton was replaced by Beaumont. Though sixth-choice lock for these Lions, Beaumont's strength and excellence in the mauls and rucks led to his inclusion in the second Test after only three provincial games and he developed into a world-class player. Cotton and Wheeler were also brought into the pack for this game and the Lions' 13–9 win was their only Test success. With Neary coming in as pack leader for the fourth and last Test, half the Lions forwards were English and it was generally agreed that the pack was not responsible for the loss of the series.

The 1977–8 season saw more law changes. Free kicks (which could be charged from ten metres) replaced penalties for certain minor offences, marks were limited to a player's side of the half-way line and the goal direct from a free kick was abolished. The last change meant the end of an era. A goal had always been permitted after a 'fair catch' (mark) but in their 345 international matches between 1871 and 1977, England had scored only four goals from a mark—by A. E. Stoddart in 1886, by E. W. Taylor in 1894, by W. G. E. Luddington in 1925 and by L. J. Corbett in 1927. The last goal from a mark against England was Don Clarke's monumental match-winner for New Zealand at Christchurch in 1963.

The 1977–8 season also saw the restructuring of English rugby as a result of Jeeps's efforts.

The County Championship, which had hitherto comprised group matches from October to December, a quarter-final in January, semi-finals in February and a final in March, was streamlined and completed by the end of December, North Midlands becoming champions for the first time.

On the first Saturday in December, 120 players started in four regional trials from which teams were selected for a Divisional Competition, won by the North under Beaumont who, after defeating London 52–6, beat the Midlands 22–7 in the final. London took third place with a 22–15 victory over the South and South West.

In addition, England Under-23, who in May and June 1977 had won all six matches on a tour of Canada, including victories over Canada by 26–13 at Ottawa and by 29–9 at Toronto, beat France Under-23 10–3 at Orrell and an England XV, led by Beaumont, the new national skipper, defeated U.S.A. 37–11 at Twickenham.

Despite this extensive programme, followed by the customary 'England *v.* The Rest' trial, only one new cap played in the first international of 1978—France at Parc des Princes. He was the Under-23 lock and captain J. P. Scott (Rosslyn Park and Devon) who filled the vacancy at number eight caused by

Uttley's injury. Like Slemen and Rafter, Scott was an ex-St Luke's, Exeter, man and it was a fitting epitaph to the College that, in their last year of independence, three of their products should play together for England in all four matches.

In the absence of Hignell, unfit, D. W. N. Caplan (Headingley) was chosen as full back but was injured in an England squad training and had to miss his first cap. He was replaced by W. H. Hare (Leicester). M. A. Burton (Gloucester) came in for Cotton, injured during the same practice week-end, and A. G. B. Old (now with Sheffield) and A. W. Maxwell (Headingley) were also recalled.

England led France 6–3 at half-time, thanks to two dropped goals by Old who thus emulated Hiller's feat against Ireland in 1970. The second was Old's third dropped goal for England and his modest three in a career enables him to share top place in England's dropped goal list with W. J. A. Davies, N. M. Hall, R. A. W. Sharp and J. F. Finlan. After half an hour England had to replace the injured Maxwell and Dixon by two more old caps, Kent and Neary, and, when Cowling dislocated a shoulder soon after the interval, he had to play on. France took control and, with two converted tries, finished victors by 15 points to 6.

Three new caps were introduced for the Welsh match at Twickenham. Two, P. W. Dodge, a nineteen-year-old, 6 foot 2 inch Leicester centre who became the first player from the England Colts team to win a full cap since it was instituted in 1973, and R. J. Mordell, a Rosslyn Park flanker, replaced injured men, but J. P. Horton, a running fly half from Bath and Lancashire, was preferred to Old. However, it was not a day for runners. Rain meant that this was one of the wettest Twickenham internationals. Conditions should have favoured England but Hignell could kick only two penalties when England had the benefit of the wind. Bennett kicked one in the first half and two in the second when the Welsh pack mastered an England eight lacking the services of Cotton and Dixon, and Wales won 9–6. The chances missed by England meant that Wales could go on to a unique third successive Triple Crown and overtake England's records of fourteen Triple Crowns and seven Grand Slams.

If the chances had been taken, England themselves could

have won the Triple Crown because the last two matches resulted in victories.

England expanded their game at Murrayfield where they beat Scotland for the first time for ten years. Caplan, a last minute inclusion for Hignell, gained the cap he had missed earlier in the season and looked a complete modern full-back with a natural positional sense and ready to attack. Lock M. J. Colclough (who had played with Beaumont in Lancashire's second row before emigrating to France and joining Angoulême) enjoyed a satisfactory debut too, and the pack, with Cotton and Dixon back, controlled the game.

After Slemen, a wing who allied deceptive speed to all-round defensive qualities, had made ground on the left, the forwards passed the ball right and Squires swerved in under the posts to score England's first try for thirteen months. The left-footed Young, who had been a soccer Blue at Cambridge and had scored 526 points in the 1975–6 season, converted with his first kick for England. Another left-footer, Dodge, celebrated his first place kick in international football with a huge penalty from three metres inside his own half, which must vie with Old's penalty at Brisbane in 1975 as the longest successful place kick in England's history.

Corless, a strong inside centre adept in set moves, slipped the ball on the scissors to the youthful Dodge and the 17 stone Cardiff loose head prop B. G. Nelmes, who had shown his mobility playing for the Barbarians against the 1977 Lions on their return from New Zealand, forced his way over for a try. Young's conversion gave England a 15–0 victory after a remarkably open game in which John Horton showed his skills by opening up in attack and by covering tackles in defence.

England retained the same side against Ireland at Twickenham and, thanks mainly to their forward control in ruck and maul, won an exciting match by 15 points to 9.

John Horton broke on the blind side and passed infield to Colclough. The admirable Dixon, in the right place at the right time as usual, was up in support to score a try which Young converted to give England a 6–0 lead at half-time.

Ward, the new Irish outside half, soon levelled the scores with a penalty goal and a dropped goal. Young put England in front again with a penalty from near the left touchline, only for Ward to make the score 9–9 with his second penalty, which brought his season's points in Five Nations Championship matches to 38, equalling the record of Roger Hosen for England in 1967 and Phil Bennett for Wales in 1976.

The match-winner was a superb try by the left winger Slemen who, having come outside the right winger Squires after Horton, Corless and Dodge had all handled, went over in the right corner. Young converted from a metre inside touch.

Mike Gibson, playing on the wing in his sixty-fifth international for Ireland, looked dangerous in the closing stages, but the England defence held. Indeed, only two tries were scored against England in 1978—both in the second half of the first match (France in Paris) when the team was hit by injuries.

Thus in 1978, as in 1977, England had again defeated both Scotland and Ireland. However, the problem of beating both Wales and France in the same season, last achieved in 1963, remained.

Statistics Section

1 England's Results in Chronological order

Season	*Opponents*	*Venue*	*Results*	
1870–1	Scotland	Raeburn Place	Lost	1T–1G 1T
1871–2	Scotland	Oval	Won	1G 1D 2T–1D
1872–3	Scotland	Partick	Drawn	0–0
1873–4	Scotland	Oval	Won	1D–1T
1874–5	Ireland	Oval	Won	1G 1D 1T–0
	Scotland	Raeburn Place	Drawn	0–0
1875–6	Ireland	Dublin	Won	1G 1T–0
	Scotland	Oval	Won	1G 1T–0
1876–7	Ireland	Oval	Won	2G 1T–0
	Scotland	Raeburn Place	Lost	0–1D
1877–8	Scotland	Oval	Drawn	0–0
	Ireland	Dublin	Won	2G 1T–0
1878–9	Scotland	Raeburn Place	Drawn	1G–1D
	Ireland	Oval	Won	2G 1D–0
1879–80	Ireland	Dublin	Won	1G 1T–1T
	Scotland	Manchester	Won	2G 3T–1G
1880–1	Ireland	Manchester	Won	2G 2T–0
	Wales	Blackheath	Won	7G 1D 6T–0
	Scotland	Raeburn Place	Drawn	1D 1T–1G 1T
1881–2	Ireland	Dublin	Drawn	2T–2T
	Scotland	Manchester	Lost	0–2T
1882–3	Wales	Swansea	Won	2G 4T–0
	Ireland	Manchester	Won	1G 3T–1T
	Scotland	Raeburn Place	Won	2T–1T
1883–4	Wales	Leeds	Won	1G 2T–1G
	Ireland	Dublin	Won	1G–0
	Scotland	Blackheath	Won	1G–1T
1884–5	Wales	Swansea	Won	1G 4T–1G 1T
	Ireland	Manchester	Won	2T–1T
1885–6	Wales	Blackheath	Won	1M 2T–1G
	Ireland	Dublin	Won	1T–0
	Scotland	Raeburn Place	Drawn	0–0
1886–7	Wales	Llanelly	Drawn	0–0
	Ireland	Dublin	Lost	0–2G
	Scotland	Manchester	Drawn	1T–1T

In above results, G=goal from try; D=dropped goal; M=goal from mark; T=unconverted try. Scoring by points was introduced in 1887–8.

Season	*Opponents*	*Venue*	*Results*	
1888–9	New Zealand Natives	Blackheath	Won	7–0
1889–90	Wales	Dewsbury	Lost	0–1
	Scotland	Raeburn Place	Won	6–0
	Ireland	Blackheath	Won	3–0

Season	*Opponents*	*Venue*	*Results*	
1890–1	Wales	Newport	Won	7–3
	Ireland	Dublin	Won	9–0
	Scotland	Richmond	Lost	3–9
1891–2	Wales	Blackheath	Won	17–0
	Ireland	Manchester	Won	7–0
	Scotland	Raeburn Place	Won	5–0
1892–3	Wales	Cardiff	Lost	11–12
	Ireland	Dublin	Won	4–0
	Scotland	Leeds	Lost	0–8
1893–4	Wales	Birkenhead	Won	24–3
	Ireland	Blackheath	Lost	5–7
	Scotland	Raeburn Place	Lost	0–6
1894–5	Wales	Swansea	Won	14–6
	Ireland	Dublin	Won	6–3
	Scotland	Richmond	Lost	3–6
1895–6	Wales	Blackheath	Won	25–0
	Ireland	Leeds	Lost	4–10
	Scotland	Hampden Park	Lost	0–11
1896–7	Wales	Newport	Lost	0–11
	Ireland	Dublin	Lost	9–13
	Scotland	Manchester	Won	12–3
1897–8	Ireland	Richmond	Lost	6–9
	Scotland	Powderhall	Drawn	3–3
	Wales	Blackheath	Won	14–7
1898–9	Wales	Swansea	Lost	3–26
	Ireland	Dublin	Lost	0–6
	Scotland	Blackheath	Lost	0–5
1899–1900	Wales	Gloucester	Lost	3–13
	Ireland	Richmond	Won	15–4
	Scotland	Inverleith	Drawn	0–0
1900–1	Wales	Cardiff	Lost	0–13
	Ireland	Dublin	Lost	6–10
	Scotland	Blackheath	Lost	3–18
1901–2	Wales	Blackheath	Lost	8–9
	Ireland	Leicester	Won	6–3
	Scotland	Inverleith	Won	6–3
1902–3	Wales	Swansea	Lost	5–21
	Ireland	Dublin	Lost	0–6
	Scotland	Richmond	Lost	6–10
1903–4	Wales	Leicester	Drawn	14–14
	Ireland	Blackheath	Won	19–0
	Scotland	Inverleith	Lost	3–6
1904–5	Wales	Cardiff	Lost	0–25
	Ireland	Cork	Lost	3–17
	Scotland	Richmond	Lost	0–8

Season	*Opponents*	*Venue*	*Results*	
1905–6	New Zealand	Crystal Palace	Lost	0–15
	Wales	Richmond	Lost	3–16
	Ireland	Leicester	Lost	6–16
	Scotland	Inverleith	Won	9–3
	France	Paris	Won	35–8
1906–7	South Africa	Crystal Palace	Drawn	3–3
	France	Richmond	Won	41–13
	Wales	Swansea	Lost	0–22
	Ireland	Dublin	Lost	9–17
	Scotland	Blackheath	Lost	3–8
1907–8	France	Paris	Won	19–0
	Wales	Bristol	Lost	18–28
	Ireland	Richmond	Won	13–3
	Scotland	Inverleith	Lost	10–16
1908–9	Australia	Blackheath	Lost	3–9
	Wales	Cardiff	Lost	0–8
	France	Leicester	Won	22–0
	Ireland	Dublin	Won	11–5
	Scotland	Richmond	Lost	8–18
1909–10	Wales	Twickenham	Won	11–6
	Ireland	Twickenham	Drawn	0–0
	France	Paris	Won	11–3
	Scotland	Inverleith	Won	14–5
1910–11	Wales	Swansea	Lost	11–15
	France	Twickenham	Won	37–0
	Ireland	Dublin	Lost	0–3
	Scotland	Twickenham	Won	13–8
1911–12	Wales	Twickenham	Won	8–0
	Ireland	Twickenham	Won	15–0
	Scotland	Inverleith	Lost	3–8
	France	Paris	Won	18–8
1912–13	South Africa	Twickenham	Lost	3–9
	Wales	Cardiff	Won	12–0
	France	Twickenham	Won	20–0
	Ireland	Dublin	Won	15–4
	Scotland	Twickenham	Won	3–0
1913–14	Wales	Twickenham	Won	10–9
	Ireland	Twickenham	Won	17–12
	Scotland	Inverleith	Won	16–15
	France	Paris	Won	39–13
1919–20	Wales	Swansea	Lost	5–19
	France	Twickenham	Won	8–3
	Ireland	Dublin	Won	14–11
	Scotland	Twickenham	Won	13–4

Season	*Opponents*	*Venue*	*Results*	
1920–1	Wales	Twickenham	Won	18–3
	Ireland	Twickenham	Won	15–0
	Scotland	Inverleith	Won	18–0
	France	Paris	Won	10–6
1921–2	Wales	Cardiff	Lost	6–28
	Ireland	Dublin	Won	12–3
	France	Twickenham	Drawn	11–11
	Scotland	Twickenham	Won	11–5
1922–3	Wales	Twickenham	Won	7–3
	Ireland	Leicester	Won	23–5
	Scotland	Inverleith	Won	8–6
	France	Paris	Won	12–3
1923–4	Wales	Swansea	Won	17–9
	Ireland	Belfast	Won	14–3
	France	Twickenham	Won	19–7
	Scotland	Twickenham	Won	19–0
1924–5	New Zealand	Twickenham	Lost	11–17
	Wales	Twickenham	Won	12–6
	Ireland	Twickenham	Drawn	6–6
	Scotland	Murrayfield	Lost	11–14
	France	Paris	Won	13–11
1925–6	Wales	Cardiff	Drawn	3–3
	Ireland	Dublin	Lost	15–19
	France	Twickenham	Won	11–0
	Scotland	Twickenham	Lost	9–17
1926–7	Wales	Twickenham	Won	11–9
	Ireland	Twickenham	Won	8–6
	Scotland	Murrayfield	Lost	13–21
	France	Paris	Lost	0–3
1927–8	New South Wales	Twickenham	Won	18–11
	Wales	Swansea	Won	10–8
	Ireland	Dublin	Won	7–6
	France	Twickenham	Won	18–8
	Scotland	Twickenham	Won	6–0
1928–9	Wales	Twickenham	Won	8–3
	Ireland	Twickenham	Lost	5–6
	Scotland	Murrayfield	Lost	6–12
	France	Paris	Won	16–6
1929–30	Wales	Cardiff	Won	11–3
	Ireland	Dublin	Lost	3–4
	France	Twickenham	Won	11–5
	Scotland	Twickenham	Drawn	0–0
1930–1	Wales	Twickenham	Drawn	11–11
	Ireland	Twickenham	Lost	5–6
	Scotland	Murrayfield	Lost	19–28
	France	Paris	Lost	13–14

Season	*Opponents*	*Venue*	*Results*	
1931–2	South Africa	Twickenham	Lost	0–7
	Wales	Swansea	Lost	5–12
	Ireland	Dublin	Won	11–8
	Scotland	Twickenham	Won	16–3
1932–3	Wales	Twickenham	Lost	3–7
	Ireland	Twickenham	Won	17–6
	Scotland	Murrayfield	Lost	0–3
1933–4	Wales	Cardiff	Won	9–0
	Ireland	Dublin	Won	13–3
	Scotland	Twickenham	Won	6–3
1934–5	Wales	Twickenham	Drawn	3–3
	Ireland	Twickenham	Won	14–3
	Scotland	Murrayfield	Lost	7–10
1935–6	New Zealand	Twickenham	Won	13–0
	Wales	Swansea	Drawn	0–0
	Ireland	Dublin	Lost	3–6
	Scotland	Twickenham	Won	9–8
1936–7	Wales	Twickenham	Won	4–3
	Ireland	Twickenham	Won	9–8
	Scotland	Murrayfield	Won	6–3
1937–8	Wales	Cardiff	Lost	8–14
	Ireland	Dublin	Won	36–14
	Scotland	Twickenham	Lost	16–21
1938–9	Wales	Twickenham	Won	3–0
	Ireland	Twickenham	Lost	0–5
	Scotland	Murrayfield	Won	9–6
1946–7	Wales	Cardiff	Won	9–6
	Ireland	Dublin	Lost	0–22
	Scotland	Twickenham	Won	24–5
	France	Twickenham	Won	6–3
1947–8	Australia	Twickenham	Lost	0–11
	Wales	Twickenham	Drawn	3–3
	Ireland	Twickenham	Lost	10–11
	Scotland	Murrayfield	Lost	3–6
	France	Paris	Lost	0–15
1948–9	Wales	Cardiff	Lost	3–9
	Ireland	Dublin	Lost	5–14
	France	Twickenham	Won	8–3
	Scotland	Twickenham	Won	19–3
1949–50	Wales	Twickenham	Lost	5–11
	Ireland	Twickenham	Won	3–0
	France	Paris	Lost	3–6
	Scotland	Murrayfield	Lost	11–13
1950–1	Wales	Swansea	Lost	5–23
	Ireland	Dublin	Lost	0–3

Season	*Opponents*	*Venue*	*Results*	
1950–1	France	Twickenham	Lost	3–11
	Scotland	Twickenham	Won	5–3
1951–2	South Africa	Twickenham	Lost	3–8
	Wales	Twickenham	Lost	6–8
	Scotland	Murrayfield	Won	19–3
	Ireland	Twickenham	Won	3–0
	France	Paris	Won	6–3
1952–3	Wales	Cardiff	Won	8–3
	Ireland	Dublin	Drawn	9–9
	France	Twickenham	Won	11–0
	Scotland	Twickenham	Won	26–8
1953–4	Wales	Twickenham	Won	9–6
	New Zealand	Twickenham	Lost	0–5
	Ireland	Twickenham	Won	14–3
	Scotland	Murrayfield	Won	13–3
	France	Paris	Lost	3–11
1954–5	Wales	Cardiff	Lost	0–3
	Ireland	Dublin	Drawn	6–6
	France	Twickenham	Lost	9–16
	Scotland	Twickenham	Won	9–6
1955–6	Wales	Twickenham	Lost	3–8
	Ireland	Twickenham	Won	20–0
	Scotland	Murrayfield	Won	11–6
	France	Paris	Lost	9–14
1956–7	Wales	Cardiff	Won	3–0
	Ireland	Dublin	Won	6–0
	France	Twickenham	Won	9–5
	Scotland	Twickenham	Won	16–3
1957–8	Wales	Twickenham	Drawn	3–3
	Australia	Twickenham	Won	9–6
	Ireland	Twickenham	Won	6–0
	France	Paris	Won	14–0
	Scotland	Murrayfield	Drawn	3–3
1958–9	Wales	Cardiff	Lost	0–5
	Ireland	Dublin	Won	3–0
	France	Twickenham	Drawn	3–3
	Scotland	Twickenham	Drawn	3–3
1959–60	Wales	Twickenham	Won	14–6
	Ireland	Twickenham	Won	8–5
	France	Paris	Drawn	3–3
	Scotland	Murrayfield	Won	21–12
1960–1	South Africa	Twickenham	Lost	0–5
	Wales	Cardiff	Lost	3–6
	Ireland	Dublin	Lost	8–11
	France	Twickenham	Drawn	5–5
	Scotland	Twickenham	Won	6–0

Season	*Opponents*	*Venue*	*Results*	
1961–2	Wales	Twickenham	Drawn	0–0
	Ireland	Twickenham	Won	16–0
	France	Paris	Lost	0–13
	Scotland	Murrayfield	Drawn	3–3
1962–3	Wales	Cardiff	Won	13–6
	Ireland	Dublin	Drawn	0–0
	France	Twickenham	Won	6–5
	Scotland	Twickenham	Won	10–8
1963	New Zealand	Auckland	Lost	11–21
	New Zealand	Christchurch	Lost	6–9
	Australia	Sydney	Lost	9–18
1963–4	New Zealand	Twickenham	Lost	0–14
	Wales	Twickenham	Drawn	6–6
	Ireland	Twickenham	Lost	5–18
	France	Paris	Won	6–3
	Scotland	Murrayfield	Lost	6–15
1964–5	Wales	Cardiff	Lost	3–14
	Ireland	Dublin	Lost	0–5
	France	Twickenham	Won	9–6
	Scotland	Twickenham	Drawn	3–3
1965–6	Wales	Twickenham	Lost	6–11
	Ireland	Twickenham	Drawn	6–6
	France	Paris	Lost	0–13
	Scotland	Murrayfield	Lost	3–6
1966–7	Australia	Twickenham	Lost	11–23
	Ireland	Dublin	Won	8–3
	France	Twickenham	Lost	12–16
	Scotland	Twickenham	Won	27–14
	Wales	Cardiff	Lost	21–34
1967–8	New Zealand	Twickenham	Lost	11–23
	Wales	Twickenham	Drawn	11–11
	Ireland	Twickenham	Drawn	9–9
	France	Paris	Lost	9–14
	Scotland	Murrayfield	Won	8–6
1968–9	Ireland	Dublin	Lost	15–17
	France	Twickenham	Won	22–8
	Scotland	Twickenham	Won	8–3
	Wales	Cardiff	Lost	9–30
1969–70	South Africa	Twickenham	Won	11–8
	Ireland	Twickenham	Won	9–3
	Wales	Twickenham	Lost	13–17
	Scotland	Murrayfield	Lost	5–14
	France	Paris	Lost	13–35
1970–1	Wales	Cardiff	Lost	6–22
	Ireland	Dublin	Won	9–6
	France	Twickenham	Drawn	14–14

Season	*Opponents*	*Venue*	*Results*	
1970–1	Scotland	Twickenham	Lost	15–16
	Scotland	Murrayfield	Lost	6–26
	Overseas XV	Twickenham	Lost	11–28
1971–2	Wales	Twickenham	Lost	3–12
	Ireland	Twickenham	Lost	12–16
	France	Paris	Lost	12–37
	Scotland	Murrayfield	Lost	9–23
1972	South Africa	Johannesburg	Won	18–9
1972–3	New Zealand	Twickenham	Lost	0–9
	Wales	Cardiff	Lost	9–25
	Ireland	Dublin	Lost	9–18
	France	Twickenham	Won	14–6
	Scotland	Twickenham	Won	20–13
1973	New Zealand	Auckland	Won	16–10
1973–4	Australia	Twickenham	Won	20–3
	Scotland	Murrayfield	Lost	14–16
	Ireland	Twickenham	Lost	21–26
	France	Paris	Drawn	12–12
	Wales	Twickenham	Won	16–12
1974–5	Ireland	Dublin	Lost	9–12
	France	Twickenham	Lost	20–27
	Wales	Cardiff	Lost	4–20
	Scotland	Twickenham	Won	7–6
1975	Australia	Sydney	Lost	9–16
	Australia	Brisbane	Lost	21–30
1975–6	Australia	Twickenham	Won	23–6
	Wales	Twickenham	Lost	9–21
	Scotland	Murrayfield	Lost	12–22
	Ireland	Twickenham	Lost	12–13
	France	Paris	Lost	9–30
1976–7	Scotland	Twickenham	Won	26–6
	Ireland	Dublin	Won	4–0
	France	Twickenham	Lost	3–4
	Wales	Cardiff	Lost	9–14
1977–8	France	Paris	Lost	6–15
	Wales	Twickenham	Lost	6–9
	Scotland	Murrayfield	Won	15–0
	Ireland	Twickenham	Won	15–9

2 England Records

(All years are for SECOND half of home season, e.g. 1974 means season 1973–4)

International Championships:

1883, 1884, 1886*, 1890*, 1892, 1910, 1912*, 1913, 1914, 1920*, 1921, 1923, 1924, 1928, 1930, 1932*, 1934, 1937, 1939*, 1947*, 1953, 1954*, 1957, 1958, 1960*, 1963, 1973*

(* indicates Championship shared)

Triple Crowns (Three Home Countries)*:*

1883, 1884, 1892, 1913, 1914, 1921, 1923, 1924, 1928, 1934, 1937, 1954, 1957, 1960

Grand Slams (Three Home Countries and France)*:*

1913, 1914, 1921, 1923, 1924, 1928, 1957

Five Wins in Season:

(Three Home Countries, France and Touring Team—New South Wales):

1928

Victories over New Zealand:

1936 (Home), 1973 (Away)

Victories over South Africa:

1970 (Home), 1972 (Away)

Victories over Australia:

1958 (Home), 1974 (Home), 1976 (Home)

World Seven-a-Side Champions:

1973

3 England's Overall Record

Opponents	*Played*	*Won*	*Drawn*	*Lost*
Scotland (1871–1978)	94	45	14	35
Ireland (1875–1978)	90	51	8	31
Wales (1881–1978)	83	33	11	39
New Zealand Natives (1889)	1	1	—	—
New Zealand (1906–73)	10	2	—	8
France (1906–78)	53	29	6	18
South Africa (1907–72)	7	2	1	4
Australia (1909–76)	9	3	—	6
New South Wales (1928)	1	1	—	—
Overseas XV (1971)	1	—	—	1
Totals	349	167	40	142

4 Most Team Points in Season

	Matches	*Con*	*Pen*	*Drop*	*Tries*	*Points*
1974	5	4	11	2	9	83
1914	4	11	—	—	20	82
1967	5	5	12	2	9	79
1924	4	7	—	1	17	69
1976	5	3	13	—	5	65
1911	4	8	2	—	13	61
1921	4	7	—	2	13	61
1971	6	2	13	1	5	61
1908	4	9	—	—	14	60
1938	3	7	4	1	10	60

5 Most Team Tries in Season

	Matches	*Tries*
1914	4	20
1881	3	18
1924	4	17
1906	5	15
1908	4	14
1913	5	14
1907	5	13
1911	4	13
1921	4	13
1928	5	13

6 Most Appearances for England

(Where possible, positions have been given modern terminology, e.g. second row forwards are listed as 'locks', wing forwards as 'flankers'.)

Name	*Seasons*	*Position(s)*	*Appearances*
J. V. Pullin	1966–76	Hooker	42
D. J. Duckham	1969–76	Centre/wing	36
D. P. Rogers	1961–9	Flanker	34
A. Neary	1971–8	Flanker	34
W. W. Wakefield	1920–7	Lock	31
E. Evans	1948–58	Prop/hooker	30
R. Cove-Smith	1921–9	Lock/prop	29
C. R. Jacobs	1956–64	Prop	29
M. P. Weston	1960–8	Centre/stand-off	29
J. Butterfield	1953–9	Centre	28
A. T. Voyce	1920–6	Flanker	27
J. S. Tucker	1922–31	Hooker	27
C. N. Lowe	1913–23	Wing	25
J. D. Currie	1956–62	Lock	25
M. S. Phillips	1958–64	Centre/wing	25
C. B. Stevens	1970–5	Prop	25
F. E. Cotton	1971–8	Prop	25
R. E. G. Jeeps	1956–62	Scrum half	24
P. J. Larter	1967–73	Lock	24
A. G. Ripley	1972–6	No. 8	24
P. J. Squires	1973–8	Wing	24
J. MacG. Kendall-Carpenter	1949–54	Prop/No. 8	23
R. W. D. Marques	1956–61	Lock	23
W. J. A. Davies	1913–23	Stand-off	22
P. E. Judd	1962–8	Prop	22
C. W. Ralston	1971–5	Lock	22
J. G. G. Birkett	1906–12	Centre	21
H. G. Periton	1925–30	Flanker	21
P. J. Dixon	1971–8	No. 8/flanker	21
P. B. Jackson	1956–63	Wing	20
R. Dibble	1906–12	Forward	19
R. J. Longland	1932–8	Prop	19
L. B. Cannell	1948–57	Centre	19
P. G. D. Robbins	1956–62	Flanker	19

Name	*Seasons*	*Position(s)*	*Appearances*
R. Hiller	1968–72	Full-back	19
C. H. Pillman	1910–14	Flanker	18
L. G. Brown	1911–22	Forward	18
E. Myers	1920–5	Centre/stand off	18
G. S. Conway	1920–7	No. 8	18
A. T. Young	1924–9	Scrum half	18
R. V. Stirling	1951–4	Prop	18
J. Roberts	1960–4	Wing	18
R. W. Poulton	1909–14	Wing/centre	17
A. F. Blakiston	1920–5	Flanker	17
N. M. Hall	1947–55	Stand off/full-back	17
P. H. Thompson	1956–9	Wing	17
R. M. Uttley	1973–7	Lock/No. 8/flanker	17
M. A. Burton	1972–8	Prop	17
E. T. Gurdon	1878–86	Forward	16
A. L. Kewney	1906–13	Forward	16
W. R. Johnston	1910–14	Full-back	16
C. A. Kershaw	1920–3	Scrum half	16
L. J. Corbett	1921–7	Centre	16
E. Stanbury	1926–9	Prop	16
C. D. Aarvold	1928–33	Centre/wing	16
W. H. Weston	1933–8	Flanker	16
P. Cranmer	1934–8	Centre/wing	16
V. G. Roberts	1947–56	Flanker	16
W. A. Holmes	1950–3	Prop	16
A. Ashcroft	1956–9	No. 8	16
J. G. Willcox	1961–4	Full-back	16
A. M. Davis	1963–70	Lock	16
R. B. Taylor	1966–71	Flanker/No. 8	16
A. G. B. Old	1972–8	Stand off	16
W. B. Beaumont	1975–8	Lock	16
H. T. Gamlin	1899–1904	Full-back	15
A. D. Stoop	1905–12	Stand off	15
J. E. Woodward	1952–6	Wing	15
D. G. Perry	1963–6	No. 8/lock	15
N. E. Horton	1969–78	Lock	15

R. Cove-Smith (22), C. N. Lowe (21), W. J. A. Davies (20) and W. W. Wakefield (20) have played on most winning England sides.

7 Most Times as England Captain

W. W. Wakefield	1924–6	13
N. M. Hall	1949–53	13
E. Evans	1956–8	13
R. E. G. Jeeps	1960–2	13
J. V. Pullin	1972–5	13
W. J. A. Davies	1921–3	11

W. J. A. Davies (10), E. Evans (9) and E. T. Gurdon (8) have captained most winning England sides.

8 Most Points in Career

		Matches	*Con*	*Pen*	*Drop*	*Tries*	*Points*
R. Hiller	1968–72	19	12	33	2	3	138
A. G. B. Old	1972–8	16	8	23	3	1	98
R. W. Hosen	1963–7	10	6	17	—	—	63
C. N. Lowe	1913–23	25	—	—	1	18	58
A. J. Hignell	1975–8	10	3	14	—	—	48
D. Lambert	1907–11	7	8	2	—	8	46
N. M. Hall	1947–55	17	8	4	3	—	39
D. Rutherford	1960–8	14	6	8	—	—	36
D. J. Duckham	1969–76	36	—	—	—	10	36
J. G. G. Birkett	1906–12	21	—	—	1	10	34
P. A. Rossborough	1971–5	7	3	7	1	1	34
B. H. Black	1930–3	10	7	4	—	2	32
A. Hudson	1906–10	8	—	—	—	10	30
R. E. Lockwood	1887–94	14	8	—	—	5	28
R. W. Poulton	1909–14	17	—	—	1	8	28
J. E. Greenwood	1912–20	13	11	2	—	—	28
C. H. Pillman	1910–14	18	1	—	—	8	26
R. A. W. Sharp	1960–7	14	4	1	3	2	26
G. S. Conway	1920–7	18	11	—	—	1	25
A. M. Smallwood	1920–5	14	—	—	1	7	25
J. F. Byrne	1894–9	12	2	4	2	—	24
W. J. A. Davies	1913–23	22	—	—	3	4	24
G. C. Robinson	1897–1901	8	—	—	—	8	24
G. W. Parker	1938	2	6	4	—	—	24
P. J. Squires	1973–8	24	—	—	—	6	24

N.B. L. Stokes (1875–81) in 12 matches, before scoring by points, had 17 conversions and 2 dropped goals.

9 Most Tries in Career

		Matches	Tries
C. N. Lowe	1913–23	25	18
J. G. G. Birkett	1906–12	21	10
A. Hudson	1906–10	8	10
D. J. Duckham	1969–76	36	10
G. C. Robinson	1897–1901	8	8
D. Lambert	1907–11	7	8
R. W. Poulton	1909–14	17	8
C. H. Pillman	1910–14	18	8
G. C. Wade	1883–6	8	7
A. M. Smallwood	1920–5	14	7
G. W. Burton	1879–81	6	6
H. H. Taylor	1879–82	5	6
W. N. Bolton	1882–7	11	6
V. H. M. Coates	1913	5	6
W. W. Wakefield	1920–7	31	6
H. C. Catcheside	1924–7	8	6
H. G. Periton	1925–30	21	6
J. E. Woodward	1952–6	15	6
P. B. Jackson	1956–63	20	6
J. Roberts	1960–4	18	6
P. J. Squires	1973–8	24	6
R. E. Lockwood	1887–94	14	5
E. F. Fookes	1896–9	10	5
A. D. Roberts	1911–14	8	5
A. T. Voyce	1920–6	27	5
H. C. C. Laird	1927–9	10	5
J. S. R. Reeve	1929–31	8	5
H. S. Sever	1936–8	10	5
R. H. Guest	1939–49	13	5
E. Evans	1948–58	30	5
J. Butterfield	1953–9	28	5
P. H. Thompson	1956–9	17	5
M. S. Phillips	1958–64	25	5
A. Neary	1971–8	34	5

10 Most Points in Season

		Matches	Con	Pen	Drop	Tries	Poin
R. Hiller	1971	5	2	12	—	3	49
R. W. Hosen	1967	5	5	12	—	—	46
A. G. B. Old	1974	5	3	9	—	1	37
R. Hiller	1969	4	3	10	—	—	36
D. Lambert	1911	3	6	2	—	2	24
C. N. Lowe	1914	4	—	—	—	8	24
G. W. Parker	1938	2	6	4	—	—	24
J. V. Richardson	1928	5	8	—	1	1	23
B. H. Black	1931	4	5	3	—	1	22
R. Hiller	1968	4	2	6	—	—	22
A. J. Hignell	1977	4	2	6	—	—	22
R. Hiller	1970	4	4	2	2	—	20
A. J. Hignell	1976	4	1	6	—	—	20
A. G. B. Old	1976	2	1	6	—	—	20
D. Rutherford	1960	4	5	3	—	—	19
V. H. M. Coates	1913	5	—	—	—	6	18
H. C. Catcheside	1924	4	—	—	—	6	18
N. M. Hall	1953	4	6	2	—	—	18
A. G. B. Old	1972	4	1	5	—	—	17
J. D. Currie	1956	4	2	4	—	—	16
P. A. Rossborough	1975	2	—	4	—	1	16
A. Hudson	1906	3	—	—	—	5	15
D. Lambert	1907	1	—	—	—	5	15
R. W. Poulton	1914	4	—	—	—	5	15
D. W. Burland	1932	2	3	2	—	1	15
A. M. Jorden	1973	3	3	3	—	—	15

N.B. L. Stokes in 1881, before scoring by points, had 8 conversions and 1 dropped goal in 3 matches.

11 Most Tries in Season

		Matches	*Tries*
C. N. Lowe	1914	4	8
V. H. M. Coates	1913	5	6
H. C. Catcheside	1924	4	6
A. Hudson	1906	3	5
D. Lambert	1907	1	5
R. W. Poulton	1914	4	5
H. H. Taylor	1881	2	4
G. W. Burton	1881	3	4
G. C. Wade	1883	3	4
J. G. G. Birkett	1908	4	4
E. R. Mobbs	1909	5	4
C. H. Pillman	1913	5	4
C. N. Lowe	1922	4	4
H. P. Jacob	1924	4	4
G. W. C. Meikle	1934	3	4
J. V. Smith	1950	4	4
D. S. Wilson	1954	5	4

12 Most Points in Match

	Opponents	Venue	Year	Con	Pen	Tries	Points
D. Lambert	France	Twick.	1911	5	2	2	22
A. G. B. Old	Ireland	Twick.	1974	1	5	—	17
P. A. Rossborough	France	Twick.	1975	—	4	1	16
D. Lambert	France	Rich.	1907	—	—	5	15d
G. W. Parker	Ireland	Dublin	1938	6	1	—	15d
R. Hiller	France	Twick.	1971	1	3	1	14*
S. A. Doble	South Africa	Jo'bg.	1972	1	4	—	14d
R. Hiller	France	Twick.	1969	2	3	—	13
A. G. B. Old	Australia	Brisbane	1975	2	3	—	13
A. Hudson	France	Paris	1906	—	—	4	12
J. E. Greenwood	France	Paris	1914	6	—	—	12
R. W. Poulton	France	Paris	1914	—	—	4	12
R. W. Hosen	Scotland	Twick.	1967	3	2	—	12
R. W. Hosen	Wales	Cardiff	1967	—	4	—	12
R. Hiller	Ireland	Dublin	1969	—	4	—	12
R. Hiller	Scotland	Twick.	1971	—	3	1	12
A. G. B. Old	Ireland	Twick.	1976	—	4	—	12*
D. W. Burland	Ireland	Dublin	1932	1	2	1	11*
H. Boughton	Ireland	Twick.	1935	1	3	—	11
R. Hiller	Overseas XV	Twick.	1971	1	2	1	11*
A. J. Hignell	Australia	Twick.	1976	1	3	—	11
E. J. Vivyan	Ireland	Black.	1904	2	—	2	10
B. C. Hill	France	Rich.	1907	5	—	—	10
R. A. W. Sharp	Ireland	Twick.	1962	2	1	1	10
A. J. Hignell	Scotland	Twick.	1977	2	2	—	10

* Indicates scored all England's points in the match.
d Indicates scored on debut for England.

N.B. In 1881, before scoring by points, L. Stokes had 6 conversions and G. W. Burton scored 4 tries *v.* Wales at Blackheath.

13 Most Tries in Match

D. Lambert	*v.* France	at Richmond	1907	5
G. W. Burton	*v.* Wales	at Blackheath	1881	4
A. Hudson	*v.* France	at Paris	1906	4
R. W. Poulton	*v.* France	at Paris	1914	4
H. H. Taylor	*v.* Ireland	at Manchester	1881	3
H. Vassall	*v.* Wales	at Blackheath	1881	3
G. C. Wade	*v.* Wales	at Swansea	1883	3
H. Marshall	*v.* Wales	at Cardiff	1893	3
V. H. M. Coates	*v.* France	at Twickenham	1913	3
C. N. Lowe	*v.* France	at Paris	1914	3
C. N. Lowe	*v.* Scotland	at Inverleith	1914	3
H. P. Jacob	*v.* France	at Twickenham	1924	3

Two Tries have been scored in a Match

v. SCOTLAND by H. H. Taylor (1880), J. G. G. Birkett (1910), C. N. Lowe (1922), J. A. Tallent (1931), J. S. R. Reeve (1931), C. D. Aarvold (1932), C. B. van Ryneveld (1949), J. V. Smith (1950), R. C. Bazley (1953), D. S. Wilson (1954), C. W. McFadyean (1967), D. J. Duckham (1969), P. J. Dixon (1973)

v. IRELAND by W. C. Hutchinson (1877), R. E. Lockwood (1891), G. C. Robinson (1900), E. J. Vivyan (1904), N. Moore (1904), A. Hudson (1908), A. C. Palmer (1909), A. D. Roberts (1912), V. H. M. Coates (1913), C. N. Lowe (1914), H. C. Catcheside (1924), A. M. Smallwood (1925), A. L. Novis (1933), H. A. Fry (1934), R. H. Guest (1948)

v. WALES by P. Christopherson (1891), S. Morfitt (1896), R. H. B. Cattell (1896), E. F. Fookes (1896), E. F. Fookes (1898), E. W. Elliott (1904), J. G. G. Birkett (1908), A. M. Smallwood (1921), H. C. Catcheside (1924), H. Wilkinson (1929), J. S. R. Reeve (1930), G. W. C. Meikle (1934), J. E. Woodward (1954), J. Roberts (1960), J. Barton (1967)

v. FRANCE by F. N. Tarr (1909), A. Hudson (1910), C. H. Pillman (1911), D. Lambert (1911), C. H. Pillman (1913), A. R. Aslett (1926), G. V. Palmer (1928), H. G. Periton (1928), P. B. Jackson (1957), P. H. Thompson (1958), D. J. Duckham (1973)

v. NEW ZEALAND NATIVES ('MAORIS') by H. Bedford (1889)

v. NEW ZEALAND by A. Obolensky (1936), R. H. Lloyd (1968)

List of England Players and Index

All years are for second half of home season (e.g. 1928 means 1927–8). Years of first and last appearances for England given, followed by position and number of appearances. Abbreviations: B = Full back, T = Three-quarter, H = Half back, F = Forward.

N.B. P. Robertshaw, threequarter, and H. Eagles, forward, were awarded caps in 1888 although they never played in an international. (See page 19.)